Printed in Canada
© Published and Copyrighted 2008 by
The Rohr Jewish Learning Institute
822 Eastern Parkway, Brooklyn, NY 11213

(888) YOUR-JLI/718-221-6900
www.myJLI.com

Talmudic Ethics

Finding Your Way to Good Decisions

JEWISH LEARNING INSTITUTE

The **Rohr Jewish Learning Institute**

gratefully acknowledges
the pioneering support of

George and Pamela Rohr

SINCE ITS INCEPTION
the **Rohr JLI** has been
a beneficiary of the vision, generosity,
care and concern
of the **Rohr family**

In the merit of
the tens of thousands of hours of Torah study
by **JLI** students worldwide
may they be blessed with health,
Yiddishe Nachas from all their loved ones,
and extraordinary success
in all their endeavors ॐ

We dedicate this course to the memory of

Mr. Herman Stern

Naftali Hertz ben Yakov ז״ל

16 Shevat 5674—4 Adar 1, 5765
February 12, 1914—February 12, 2005

In honor of his third *Yahrtzeit*

Generous of heart and beloved by all
Pillar of the Lubavitch on the Palisades Community, Tenafly, New Jersey

May the study of Torah be an everlasting monument to his name.

Endorsements for
Talmudic Ethics
Finding Your Way to **Good Decisions**

The JLI program admirably merges Torah learning with American jurisprudence. It encourages Talmudic scholars and beginners to appreciate American law and stimulates lawyers and laymen to treasure the wisdom of the Torah.

Nathan Lewin
Honorary President of the American Association of Jewish Lawyers and Jurists

Leadership is in a crisis—from business to government, from religious institutions to the UN, leaders have lost their moral compass. The Rohr JLI course offers 21st-century leaders of all stripes a crucial lighthouse in the sea of ethical uncertainty. Thank you and keep up the good work.

Thomas D. Zweifel
CEO, Swiss Consulting Group and Professor of Leadership, Columbia University

Talmudic Ethics

Finding Your Way to Good Decisions

The course
**Talmudic
Ethics**
has been approved
in these states
for fulfillment of
the requirements for
continuing legal education

Alabama
California
Colorado
Delaware
Florida
Georgia
Illinois
Indiana
Minnesota
Missouri
Nevada
North Carolina
New Mexico
Ohio
Oregon
Oklahoma
Pennsylvania
Rhode Island
South Carolina
Tennessee
Virginia
Washington
Wisconsin

ACCREDITED
CLE
FOR ATTORNEYS

Table of Contents

Talmudic Ethics

Finding Your Way to Good Decisions

Lesson 1
My Brother, Myself
Saving Yourself vs. Saving Others

Introduction

A problem currently making the rounds in academic circles is this:

A trolley is running out of control down a track. In its path are five people who have been tied to the track by a mad philosopher. Fortunately, you can flip a switch which will lead the trolley down a different track to safety. Unfortunately, there is one person tied to that track. Should you flip the switch?

What is our obligation to others, and to ourselves? Can we ever sacrifice one life to save many others? What principles can help us solve these kinds of problems?

These questions are the subject of the first lesson.

Overview of Jewish Ethics: Rights vs. Responsibilities

Learning Exercise 1

Read the following question asked of a rabbi during the Holocaust:

The Case:

A father of a fifteen-year-old boy came to me and asked the following question: The SS had just rounded up fourteen hundred boys, between the ages of fourteen and eighteen, to be killed on the following day, including his son. The father, however, managed to convince one of the guards to release his son in exchange for a large bribe. He wanted to know whether he was permitted to save his son since, as a result, the officer would round up another child in order to maintain the quota.

RABBI TZVI HIRSH MEISELS, MEKADSHEI HASHEM, VOL. I, PAGE 8

Rabbi Tzvi Hirsh Meisels (1904–1974), Weitzener *Rav,* Rabbi of Vác, Hungary, and author of *Mekadshei HaShem* and *Binyan Zion,* served as spiritual mentor to thousands in Auschwitz.

Questions for Discussion

1. How do you think you might have answered this question?

2. What reasons might you give for your answer?

3. What does the very fact that the question was asked tell you about the father of the boy?

Learning **Exercise 2**

Below are two justifications for ethical behavior:

We hold these truths to be self-evident, that all men are created equal, that they are endowed by their Creator with certain inalienable Rights, that among these are Life, Liberty, and the pursuit of Happiness.

That to secure these rights, Governments are instituted among Men, deriving their just powers from the consent of the Governed, . . .

UNITED STATES DECLARATION OF INDEPENDENCE

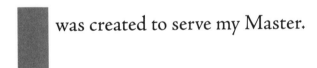 ואני נבראתי לשמש את קוני

I was created to serve my Master.

TALMUD, KIDUSHIN 82A

Questions for Discussion

1. According to the Declaration of Independence, why would it be wrong to harm others?

2. According to the Talmud, why would it be wrong to harm others?

The Obligation to Save the Life or Property of Another Person

Text 1a 🔲

לֹא תַעֲמֹד עַל דַּם רֵעֶךָ

Do not stand idly by the blood of your fellow.

VAYIKRA/LEVITICUS 19:16

Text 1b 🔲

מנין לרואה את חברו שהוא טובע בנהר או חיה גוררתו או לסטין באין עליו
שהוא חייב להצילו?
תלמוד לומר "לא תעמד על דם רעך"
והא מהכא נפקא? מהתם נפקא: אבדת גופו מניין?
תלמוד לומר: "והשבתו לו"
אי מהתם הוה אמינא: הני מילי בנפשיה
אבל מיטרח ומיגר אגורי, אימא לא, קא משמע לן

How do we know that if someone sees his friend drowning in the river or being dragged by a wild animal or being attacked by gangsters that one is obligated to save him? Because it says: "Do not stand idly by the blood of your fellow."

[But] don't we learn this from another place in the Torah? As we have learned: How do we know that one has an obligation to restore another's life [saving him in case of danger]? Because it says: "And you shall surely return his lost property (Devarim/Deuteronomy 22:2)."

[It already mentions earlier in the text that one is required to guard lost property which one finds until the owner of the lost property is identified. The repetition (See 22:1-2) of the obligation to return that which is someone else's alludes to the obligation to restore one's life.]

[The Talmud answers:] From the juxtaposition to the obligation to lost property alone, it would seem that one must only save another's life with one's own body [efforts], but there is no requirement to spend money to save another's life.

[i.e., just as one is not required to spend one's own money to save someone else's property.]

This is why we need the verse: "Do not stand idly by the blood of your fellow," to teach that one is required to spend his own financial resources to save a life.

TALMUD, SANHEDRIN 73A

Chart 1

Torah Verse	Implication
You shall surely return his lost property (Devarim 22:2).	You must save someone from loss if you can, but need not incur personal expense to do so.
Do not stand idly by the blood of your fellow (Vayikra 19:16).	In order to prevent loss of life, you are even obligated to incur personal expense.

The Obligation to Save Your Own Life

Text 2

Rabbi Yehudah HeChasid of Regensburg (1150-1217) was a Talmudic scholar, mystic, and Kabbalist. He was the leader of *Chasidei Ashkenaz,* a pietistic group of scholars and mystics. He wrote *Sefer Chasidim* (*"Book of the Pious"*), a guidebook of the religious life of medieval German Jews. Many of his teachings and customs have been incorporated into standard Halachic Jewish practice.

"However, your blood which belongs to your souls I will demand . . . . " This teaches us that if a man dies by his own neglect—for instance, if he engages in quarrels which eventually lead to his own fatality—he will be accountable to G-d for causing his own death. Or if someone walks in a place of danger, such as walking on a frozen lake in the winter, and subsequently drowns, or if someone engages in a provocation with a killer . . . about all these it says: "Your blood which belongs to your souls I will demand."

RABBI YEHUDAH HECHASID, SEFER CHASIDIM, NO. 675

Competing Interests: Whose Life Comes First?

If Both People Are in Equal Danger

Text 3

שנים שהיו מהלכין בדרך וביד אחד מהן קיתון של מים
אם שותין שניהם, מתים ואם שותה אחד מהן, מגיע לישוב
דרש בן פטורא: "מוטב שישתו שניהם וימותו
ואל יראה אחד מהם במיתתו של חבירו"
עד שבא רבי עקיבא ולימד: "וחי אחיך עמך"
חייך קודמים לחיי חבירך

Two people are walking along the way, and one of them holds a flask of water in his hand. If both of them drink, they will die; but if one of them drinks, he will reach the safety of civilization. Ben Petora expounded: It is better that both of them should drink and die, and so that neither of them will see the death of his fellow. Until Rabbi Akiva came and taught: "That your brother may live with you"—your life takes precedence over any other life. [Rabbi Akiva interprets "with you" as meaning "secondary to you."]

TALMUD, BAVA METSIA 62A

If the Other Person Is
in Greater Need Than You

Text 4

מעיין של בני העיר: חייהן וחיי אחרים: חייהן קודמין לחיי אחרים
בהמתם ובהמת אחרים: בהמתם קודמת לבהמת אחרים
כביסתן וכביסת אחרים: כביסתן קודמת לכביסת אחרים
חיי אחרים וכביסתן: חיי אחרים קודמין לכביסתן

When a stream that originates in one town flows through another and does not provide enough drinking water for both towns, the water rights belong to the inhabitants of the first town. The same applies to water that both need for their livestock or for washing their clothes. If, however, the second town needs drinking water for its citizens, while the first town only needs the water for washing clothes, then the needs of the second town prevail.

Talmud, Nedarim 80b

Text 5

The hardships of these times are not hidden from me, in that the means for earning a livelihood have declined, especially among those known to me from your community, whose hands have faltered so that they are without any providers at all (with no work available for either husband or wife), and they literally borrow in order to eat. May G-d show them compassion and speedily bring them respite from their straits.

Nonetheless, they are not acting rightly unto their souls, according to reports that they close their hand which all their life long, to this very day, has been open to give with a full hand and a generous eye for all vital necessities to satisfy the needs of the "clean" destitutes whose eyes are lifted unto us. If we will not pity them, Heaven forfend, who will? And it is written, " . . . so that your brother may live with you!"

As to the ruling of the Sages that "Your own life takes precedence," this applies only in the case "when one has a pitcher of water in his hand;" that is, when it is equally essential that both drink in order to save their lives from thirst. But if a pauper needs bread for the mouths of babes, and firewood and clothes against the cold, and the like, then all these take precedence over any fine apparel and family feasts, with meat and fish and all kinds of delicacies, for oneself and all of one's household. The rule that "your own life takes precedence" does not apply in such a case, because these are not really essential to life, as are the needs of the poor, in true equality, as is discussed in *Nedarim*, page 8ob.

RABBI SHNE'UR ZALMAN OF LIADI, IGERET HAKODESH, CH. 16

Rabbi Shne'ur Zalman of Liadi (1745–1813), "the Alter Rebbe," author of *Tanya*, an early classic of Chassidism; *Torah Or; Likutei Torah;* and *Shulchan Aruch HaRav,* a halachic commentary. He founded the Chabad school of mysticism.

If You Must Enter a Dangerous Situation to Save Another Person

Text 6

רבי איסי איתצייד בספסופה

אמר רבי יונתן: "יכרך המת בסדינו"

אמר רבי שמעון בן לקיש: "עד דאנא קטיל ואנא מיתקטיל
אנא איזיל ומשיזיב ליה בחיילא"

אזל ופייסון ויהבוניה ליה

R abbi Isi was caught by a group of robbers. Rabbi Yonatan said [upon hearing the news about R. Isi]: "Let us prepare some shrouds for R. Isi." Resh Lakish said: "Either I will be killed by them or they will be killed by me. I am going to save him from their hands!" Resh Lakish met with them and succeeded in negotiating R. Isi's release.

JERUSALEM TALMUD, TERUMOT 8:4

If You Must Kill Someone Else to Save Yourself

Text 7

כי ההוא דאתא לקמיה דרבא

אמר ליה: "מרי דוראי אמר לי זיל קטליה לפלניא

ואי לא, קטלינא לך"

אמר ליה: "ליקטלוך ולא תיקטול

מאי חזית דדמא דידך סומק טפי?

דילמא דמא דההוא גברא סומק טפי?"

A certain individual came before Rava and said to him, "The governor of my town said to me, 'Go kill so-and-so, and if you do not kill him, I will kill you.' What shall I do?"

Rava said to him: "Let him kill you, and do not kill anyone, for what makes you assume that your blood is redder than that of your victim? Perhaps the blood of that man whom they want you to kill is redder than yours!"

Talmud, Pesachim 25b

Question for Discussion

Why does your own life take precedence in Text 3 (when there is only one flask of water in the desert) but not in Text 7?

If You Must Kill Someone Else to Prevent Him from Killing You—*Rodef*

Text 8 ▌

אבל הרודף אחר חבירו להרגו אפילו היה הרודף קטן
הרי כל ישראל מצווין להציל הנרדף מיד הרודף ואפילו בנפשו של רודף

כיצד, אם הזהירוהו והרי הוא רודף אחריו אף על פי שלא קיבל עליו התראה
כיון שעדיין הוא רודף הרי זה נהרג
ואם יכולים להצילו באבר מאיברי הרודף
כגון שיכו אותו בחץ או באבן או בסייף
ויקטעו את ידו או ישברו את רגלו או יסמו את עינו, עושין

All Israel is commanded to save a person whose life is being pursued, even if it means killing the pursuer, and even if the pursuer is a minor.

Thus, if warning is issued, and he continues to pursue, the pursuer can be killed even without his acknowledging the warning.

But if the pursuer can be stopped by disabling part of his body, whether by striking him with an arrow, a stone, or a sword, or by cutting off his hand, breaking his leg, or blinding him, then that should be done . . . .

RAMBAM (MAIMONIDES)
MISHNEH TORAH, HILCHOT ROTZEACH (LAWS OF MURDER) 1:6-7

R. Moshe ben Maimon (1135–1204), better known as Maimonides or Rambam, author of *Mishneh Torah*, a compendium of Jewish law, and *Guide for the Perplexed*. He was born in Córdoba, Spain. After the conquest of Córdoba by the Almohads, who sought to forcibly convert the Jews to Islam, he fled and eventually settled in Cairo. There he became the leader of the Jewish community and served as court physician to the vizier of Egypt.

If an Individual Must be Sacrificed to Save a Group

Text 9

וכן אם אמרו להם עובדי כוכבים
תנו לנו אחד מכם ונהרגנו ואם לאו נהרוג כולכם
יהרגו כולם ואל ימסרו להם נפש אחת מישראל

A group of people are told by a band of gangsters: "Give us one of you and we will kill him, and if you refuse we will kill all of you." The law is: let them all be killed, but they should not deliver even a single soul to enemy hands.

RAMBAM, HILCHOT YESODEI HATORAH
(LAWS OF THE FOUNDATIONS OF TORAH) 5:5

Question for Discussion

In Text 7, we established that you have no right to kill someone else to save yourself, as your life is not more important than his.

But in this case, no one is swapping their own life for another person's; if the person is not handed over, everyone will die! Why shouldn't it be permitted to sacrifice the life of one who will not survive anyway in order to save a whole group? Why should everyone else die unnecessarily?

Resolution of Learning Exercise 1 (Holocaust Case)

Text 10 📖

המלך או שר שמטיל איזה דבר על עשיר א׳ או ב׳
ויש ליהודי א׳ כח בהיכל המלך והשר להשתדל לפוטרם
אם הדבר ברור ודאי שאם יפטרם לאלו יטיל על אחרים
אי רשאי להצילם לאלו או לא
פסק בתשו׳ מהריב״ל חלק ב׳ סימן מ׳ דאם כבר הטיל המלך על אנשים ידועים
ופרט אותם ונלכדו ברשתו
אזי אין יהודי רשאי להשתדל לפוטרן בשום ענין שיזיק לאחרים בודאי
אבל אם יצא גזרה להטיל על ב׳ אנשים בסתם
יכול יהודי להשתדל על איזה אנשים שרוצה שלא יהיו בכלל הגזירה
אף שבודאי יכנסו אחרים

Rabbi Shabetai ben Meir HaKohen (1621–1662), was a leading halachic authority. At a very young age, he was appointed to the Vilna *Beit Din*. The most famous of his numerous compositions is *Siftei Kohen* ("*Shach*"), one of the most important commentaries on *Shulchan Aruch Yoreh De'ah*, which he published in 1646 at 24. He also wrote a very important commentary on *Shulchan Aruch, Choshen Mishpat*.

I f a king or a ruler imposed a draft to royal service upon two prominent members of the Jewish community, and another Jew is able to intervene on their behalf (by using his special connections to government officials), is he permitted to do so, knowing that the king might draft two other Jews instead?

Rabbi ben Lev ruled that if the king had already specified the individuals for this draft, then one may not intervene on their behalf and cause others to face this ordeal. However, if the king merely issued an edict that two Jewish members of the community must be taken into custody for this service, then it is permitted to ensure that individuals who are important to the community will not become victims of this draft.

RABBI SHABETAI KOHEN, SIFTEI KOHEN, CHOSHEN MISHPAT 163:18

Text 11 📜

ראה אמת המים שוטפת ובאה לתוך שדהו
עד שלא נכנסו המים לתוך שדהו רשאי לפנותן למקום אחר
משנכנסו אין רשאי לפנותן למקום אחר

f a man sees a flood of water coming down towards his field, he is permitted to shut the gate to his field, causing the water to divert in another direction, even though the water will flood his neighbor's field. However, if the water has already entered his field, he may not move the water out of it, causing the water to go to his neighbor's field.

RABBI YOSEF KARO, SHULCHAN ARUCH, CHOSHEN MISHPAT 388:2

Rabbi Yosef Karo (1488–1575), author of the *Shulchan Aruch* (a definitively authoritative code of Jewish law); *Beit Yosef,* a commentary on *Arba'ah Turim;* on Jewish law; *Kesef Mishneh* on Maimonides' *Mishneh Torah;* and a mystical work, *Magid Mesharim.* Born in Spain, he fled the Inquisition at the age of four with his family.

Text 12 📜

t seems that Rabbi ben Lev's ruling only applies to others who wish to intervene and save those who have already been drafted by the king. However, one of the individual draftees is permitted to do everything in his power to save himself, even though this may cause others to take his place, as we have the principle of "your life comes first."

RABBI AVRAHAM MASKIL LE'EITAN, YAD AVRAHAM, YOREH DE'AH 157

Key Points

1. Ethics in Judaism is about obligations, not rights.

2. In general, we are morally obligated to preserve the lives of others, even to the extent of incurring financial loss ourselves.

3. When we must make a choice between saving ourselves or another person in equal danger, our first obligation is to save ourselves.

4. One should be willing to endure inconvenience to save another person who is in greater need.

5. One need not place oneself in danger to save another person.

6. One is generally forbidden to kill another person in order to save one's own life.

7. However, one is obligated to protect oneself against a threatening aggressor (*rodef*).

8. In triage situations, one may use rational considerations in deciding who to save first. However, one is never allowed to actively sacrifice the life of an innocent individual, even for the sake of a large group.

9. The dichotomy between self and others is a false one. These laws reflect a deep respect for the infinite value of every life and our responsibility to preserve all lives, including our own, which have been given to us in trust.

Additional Readings

"So One May Live"— Siamese Twins

Unpublished Responsum by Rav Moshe Feinstein, *zt"l*
Translated and Annotated by Rabbi Moshe Dovid Tendler

Early in September, 1977, a drama began that added much kavod, much dignity, to the wisdom of Torah and to those who spend their lives applying Torah knowledge to the complex problems encountered daily in the modern world. In Lakewood, New Jersey, Siamese twins were born to a prestigious family of Torah educators. The twins were taken by helicopter, on September 15, to the Children's Hospital in Philadelphia, where Dr. C. Everett Koop, who subsequently became the Surgeon General of the United States, was then the hospital's Chief of Surgery. Immediately after the initial evaluation, it was obvious to all the physicians called in to evaluate the twins that both would die unless they were separated. However, the only way one child would be viable was if the other child was killed during surgery. The question was referred to Rav Moshe Feinstein for his evaluation and decision.

The children, designated Baby A and Baby B, were fused in the ventral area all the way from the shoulder down to the pelvic region. The twins shared one six-chambered heart. The wall separating the essentially normal four chambers from the other two, most likely the stunted heart of Baby A, was too thin to be divided. It was not possible to give the two chambered heart to Baby A, so that she would survive for as long as a two-chambered heart could carry her physiological needs. There was only one solution. The entire six-chambered heart had to be given to Baby B, and the life of Baby A would have to be sacrificed.

It was clear to all concerned that this was a major ethical issue that had ramifications for the abortion debate, and for the ethics of neonate salvage. The Chief Surgeon, a deeply religious man, was fully aware of the ethical import of any decision in this case. Dr. Koop referred the case to the courts so as not to have any accusation of premeditated murder leveled against him. In addition, nurses and doctors at Children's Hospital consulted with their religious guides, and many reported back that they would not be able to participate in the surgery.

On September 20, I met with Dr. Koop and his staff to determine the medical facts. The first halachic concern was to establish that we were, in fact, dealing with two separate human beings. Although they were joined at the chest and their livers were co-joined, as were the hearts, the girls were separate human beings with their own brains and nervous systems. Dr. Koop recommended that the twins should be separated as soon as possible, because there were signs that the heart was failing and could not maintain the load of supplying blood to two infants. It was emphasized that even with surgery the chance was slim that one could be saved. Never before had Siamese twins been successfully separated from a ventral connection, and certainly not when they had a joined liver and a single heart between them.

On September 30, twenty doctors and nurses assembled in the meeting room to be brought up to date. Many were already disturbed by the lapse of time. They were all leaders in their fields and had gathered to be able to participate in the separation. Practically every surgical and medical specialty was represented, since no one really knew, despite the X-rays and the many tests that had been done, what they would encounter during actual surgery. Dr. Koop had prepared a team that would be able to handle any emergency that might arise. In brainstorming sessions, all possible problems were discussed. The simple problem of fitting a six-chambered heart into the small chest of Baby B proved to be unexpectedly difficult and could be resolved only by building the chest larger by using part of the chest of Baby A. On October 3, the intensive care unit nurse assigned to the twins noticed significant changes in the heart rate and respiration and in the electrocardiograph tracings. This was reported to Rav Feinstein, who then posed, once again, the key question: Was Dr. Koop sure that the six-chambered heart could only be given to Baby B? Could it not also be given to Baby A and have Baby B die?

Dr. Koop responded that there was no doubt that the only infant who could be helped by surgery was Baby B, because in addition to the shared liver and heart, Baby A also had a circulatory defect that would not permit her to survive any length of time, even if she were given the six-chambered heart.

Discussion involved many members of the Feinstein/ Tendler family, each contributing his own insight. The surgical team had essentially completed its work and had a plan which allowed for the separation of the twins despite the unknown consequences of the separation. If Baby A was to be sacrificed, it was important that the separation be done immediately after Baby A was no longer alive, so that the toxins that immediately pour out when tissue is devitalized would not begin to affect the survival of Baby B. Yet there was little knowledge as to what impact the sudden removal of a large volume of blood (the blood that was circulating in Baby A) would have on the functioning of the six-chambered heart now in Baby B's chest.

On October 6, Rav Feinstein asked me to call Dr. Koop and instruct him to go ahead with the surgery. On Tuesday, October 11, the surgery was completed. Baby B successfully survived the surgery. Baby A had to be sacrificed. The following is a summation of Rav Moshe's reasoning for approving the surgery. A second approach that leads to the same conclusion, but based upon a different halachic principle, is also here recorded since it was presented in great detail during the discussions that led to the final permissive ruling.

One of the fundamental rules of halachah is that one life is not to be sacrificed for another. An exception to this rule is the sacrifice of a fetus in order to save the life of the mother during delivery. The Mishnah in Ohalos [7:61] records: "If a woman is in difficulty during childbirth, it is permissible to destroy the fetus surgically because her life comes first. If, however, the head of the fetus has already been delivered, then it is forbidden to intercede even though it may cost the life of the mother. The fetus is now an infant with the ability for independent life. Therefore, we do not sacrifice one life to save another."

The Talmud in Sanhedrin [72b] elaborates on this mishnah by posing the question: "Why should you not sacrifice the infant even though the head has already been presented, since this infant is endangering the life of the mother? Is not the infant, then, a rodef [pursuer]? The law of the pursuer should apply, which is to kill the pursuer in order to save the life of the victim." The Talmud answers: "No, Heaven is the pursuer." In other words, this is an act of Hashem, and therefore it is not correct to assume that

the fetus is the attacker. We cannot decide to favor either the child or the mother in this terrible dilemma. While the child is in the uterine environment, totally dependent on the mother's life yet threatening it, we classify the fetus as a pursuer. The logic is, as Maimonides says, "simple." While in the uterine environment, the child is totally dependent on the mother's life forces. Thus, either the mother's death or the fetus's death would result in a fetus that was not viable. This complete dependency on the mother, so that if the mother dies the fetus will also die, is the reason for giving the mother priority over the fetus, because she is the source of fetal life.

Once the head appears, however, and the child is able to breathe independently, he is treated as an entity separate from the mother. He is now independent of the mother's circulatory and respiratory systems. We grant him the full rights and privileges of an adult. The most important of these privileges is the right to life.

This is surely the Rambam's reasoning in Laws of Murder [1:91]. The Rambam states as follows: "When the head has appeared we no longer intervene because we cannot destroy one life for the sake of another." He adds the explanation: "For this is natural law." Why is this case less a matter of natural law than when the fetus is still in utero? Why do we not say that "Heaven is the pursuer," and not intervene, even in early pregnancy? It is, after all, an "act of Heaven"? Surely, it is the fetal status of dependency on the mother that justifies the sacrifice of fetal life to save maternal life.

Rav Feinstein compared the case of the Siamese twins to this classic case of the conflict for survival between a mother in childbirth and the fetus. Baby A had no independent ability to survive. Her entire survival was completely dependent on her sister, who had the circulatory system to back up the functioning of the heart and liver.

To Rav Feinstein's critical question, "Can the heart be given to Baby A and she would live?" Dr. Koop had responded, "No, there is no way to save Baby A. The issue is only should both die or should Baby B be saved." Without the attempted separation, both would surely die, and therefore in halachic terminology we classify the baby that had no independent survival, Baby A, as the pursuer, as if she were pursuing her sister and threatening her life.

Further, sophisticated testing had determined that the halachic concept of dependency was, indeed, the relationship between the twins. The two-chambered heart, which was the heart of Baby A, was receiving its blood though two apertures leaking from the four-chambered heart. Except for that contribution of blood to the two chambers Baby A would have died in utero. This was the analysis that allowed the surgery to proceed.

I recall how impressed I was with a statement Dr. Koop made, a statement that in my opinion revealed the man's personality and also incurred a special merit. When the team of twenty or so professionals were awaiting Rav Feinstein's decision, and, indeed, were expressing impatience at the lapse of time, which interfered with their private, professional lives significantly, Dr. Koop quieted the group with the following statement: "The ethics and morals involved in this decision are too complex for me. I believe they are too complex for you as well. Therefore I referred it to an old rabbi on the Lower East Side of New York. He is a great scholar, a saintly individual. He knows how to answer such questions. When he tells me, I too will know."

During the almost two weeks of intensive discussions held under the guidance of Rav Moshe, an objection was raised to the analogy to a mother in difficult childbirth. The Rambam uses the expression: "For this is tivo shel olam, or the law of nature, or more accurately, the natural event of our world."

It is easy to see how such an expression applies to a woman in childbirth, since childbirth, a normal natural event, sometimes involves dangers that result in a serious conflict between the mother and the child about to be brought into the world. It is difficult to see how this concept can be applied to so rare an occurrence—birth of a Siamese twin, especially one with a six-chambered heart and a shared liver, as was our case. Therefore, a second approach was suggested which received the careful attention of Rav Moshe. It did not receive his concurrence, only his appreciation for the analysis suggested.

The Talmud in Sanhedrin [72b] and the commentary of Rashi on the case of Sheva ben Bichri recorded in II Samuel 20:

There was an evil man named Sheva ben Bichri ... and he said, "I have no allegiance to David HaMelech" [i.e., he led a rebellion against King David]. Yoav's men chased after him and they came to a town and laid siege to it. Yoav announced to the townspeople, "Sheva ben Bichri has raised his hand against David HaMelech. Send him out of your town, for he alone is the one that is guilty, and I will then withdraw my forces from the siege." A woman responded to Yoav, "Behold, here is his head which I am throwing to you next to the walls of the city."

The whole story is cited in great detail in the Talmud Yerushalmi, Terumot [8:41]. From this story is derived a halachic ruling concerning a caravan of Jews surrounded by gentiles. The gentiles had the military power to destroy the Jews but instead offered a deal: "If you will give us one of you so that we may do as we will with him and kill him, then you can all go free. If not, we will kill you all."

The Talmud rules that it is forbidden to hand over one Jewish life to them even though all must forfeit their lives. If, however, the gentiles had singled out one individual against whom they had some complaint, as specified: "Give us this man," just as in the case of Sheva ben Bichri, the halachah states that he should be turned over to them and the entire caravan be saved.

Resh Lakish qualifies this ruling by saying that it applies only if he is guilty of a death penalty, as was Sheva ben Bichri, who rebelled against the king and incurred such a penalty. Rav Yochanan states that this is not a prerequisite. Even if he was not guilty, as long as they specified "this man and this man alone," it is permitted to turn him over in order to save the rest. Rashi, in his commentary on Sanhedrin, analyzes the case further and points out that whereas it was permissible to turn over Sheva ben Bichri, it is not permissible to kill a fetus which has already presented its head so that there is independent life, because sacrificing one life for another is forbidden. In the case of Sheva ben Bichri, even if they had not handed him over, they would not have been able to protect him against the siege laid by Yoav. They could only have died with him. If, however, there had been a possibility that defending him would have given him an opportunity to escape, so that there was no certainty that he would die, then they would have been required to raise a defense, and not save themselves by causing the death of Sheva ben Bichri.

The Rambam, in Law of the Foundations of Torah [5:5], concludes that Resh Lakish's opinion, and not Rav Yochanan's, is the correct one: "If he is liable to the penalty of death, as was Sheva ben Bichri, they are permitted to turn him over in order to save themselves. If, however, he is not guilty of any death penalty, then it is forbidden to turn him over, but they must defend themselves and him even if it means forfeiting all their lives."

It is clear, according to Rashi's analysis in his commentary on Sanhedrin, that in our case, where both would have died, it was permissible to sacrifice one in order to save the other. But according to Maimonides's ruling, unless one of them had incurred the penalty of death, it was forbidden to do so. The Rema, in Yoreh De'ah 157, records the Rambam's ruling as the correct halachah that it is forbidden to save one life at the cost of another unless that individual was guilty of a death penalty, as was the case of Sheva ben Bichri.

The analysis of the case of the Siamese twins, however, seems to satisfy even the requirement of Maimonides, so that in this case all would have concurred with the opinion of Rav Moshe. Baby A could not live, no matter what surgical plan was followed. Although there was no ruling of a Beit Din that she was guilty of any sin and therefore would be subjected to capital punishment, Hashem Himself issued such a ruling. There was an edict from Heaven that the child could not live. Nobody could help this child. Even if all the organs were placed in her body, she could not survive. Therefore, Baby A should be classified as if she were Sheva ben Bichri, for whom there was no hope, and the destiny was already inscribed by Hashem Himself, that this soul would enter the world only for a limited period of time so as to "help empty the storehouse of souls and hasten the coming of Moshiach" (Yevamot 62a).

The decision to sacrifice her is one that would have had the approval of both Rashi and the Rambam. The logic of equating inevitable death from physiological causes, because of the anatomical deficiencies of Baby A, and a case in which an individual is guilty of a capital crime, is based on an analysis by the Rema in Sanhedrin 72b, and I quote: "The case of the woman in labor requires deep analysis. The fetus was not guilty of any crime. It is like the case of a caravan surrounded by enemies in which the gentiles demand one life in order to let the other go, where the ruling is that we may not sacrifice one life even to save many lives." The Rema concludes [that the rule that "we do not sacrifice one life even to save many lives" applies] only because the fetus has a chance to live. If the fetus did not have a chance to live, there would be no problem about killing it to save the mother, because the absence of any hope that the fetus could survive, and not the mother, makes it as if this individual were designated for death. According to Rema's analysis, then, in an early pregnancy, where the child still does not have viability, it is tantamount to being designated for death. Thus, in our case, Baby A, because of the defects in her body structure, had been designated for death, and therefore it is permissible to hasten that death in order to save the life of the sister.

Excerpted with permission from:
Care of the Critically Ill, Vol. 1, by Rabbi Moshe Tendler
http://www.jlaw.com/Articles/ravmoshe.html

Reprinted with permission from JLaw.com

Lesson 2
The Ebbing Flame
Jewish Perspectives on Euthanasia

Introduction

ach Dunlap was pronounced dead on November 19, 2007 at a hospital in Texas, after he was injured in an all-terrain vehicle accident. His family approved having his organs harvested for transplant.

As family members were paying their last respects, he moved his foot and hand. He reacted to a pocketknife scraped across his foot and to pressure applied under a fingernail. After forty-eight days in the hospital, he was allowed to return home, where he continues to work on his recovery.

Four months after he was declared brain dead and doctors were about to remove his organs for transplant, Dunlap says he feels "pretty good."

What is this mystery called life? Where does it come from? How does it end? How can we detect its presence? To what point must we preserve it? And how can we tell when it is finally gone? These questions are the subject of our lesson.

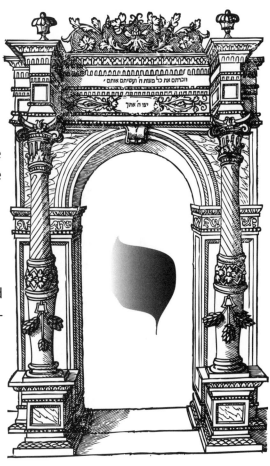

General Introduction to Jewish Medical Ethics
Case Studies about the End of Life

Learning **Activity**

Case **Study 1**

The Esteemed Rabbi Shlomo Zalman Auerbach,

I have some patients who suffer from terminal cancer. The excruciating pain they live with is unrelenting. In medical clinics around the world, it is acceptable to provide strong pain killers such as morphine that are highly effective in easing the pain. The question I have is that it is almost certain that these pain killers will lead to the shortening of the patient's life, although they are not provided for that purpose. This is because due to the weak state of the patients, the medications weaken their respiratory system, thereby greatly increasing their risk of contracting pneumonia, which can lead to the death of the patient.

I am quite sure that if we compare the outcomes of patients who did get morphine with those who did not, we would find that the mortality rate among those who did get morphine is much higher.

Despite this fact, I have never encountered a physician who would question the ethics of administering these pain killers in order to lighten the suffering of the patient. My question to you, esteemed Rabbi, is: What does Jewish law have to say with regard to this question?

Dr. Shimon Glick, Head of the Internal Unit, Central Hospital of the Negev/Be'er Sheva

RABBI SHLOMO ZALMAN AUERBACH, ATERET SHLOMO, VOL. 7, P.III

Rabbi Shlomo Zalman Auerbach (1910–1995) of Jerusalem was recognized as one of the prominent halachic authorities of his time. Many of his decisions and works related to the halachic problems that arose with the introduction of modern technology.

Case **Study 2**

Dear Rabbi Feinstein,

I have a patient who is terminally ill. There is very little we can do to relieve him from his unbearable suffering. Are we required to provide the patient with remedies which, while not providing a cure, will delay his death for a period of time, or is it better that he dies sooner?

Dr. N. Z. Ringel

RABBI MOSHE FEINSTEIN, IGEROT MOSHE
CHOSHEN MISHPAT, VOL. 2, NO. 73

Rabbi Moshe Feinstein (1895–1986). He studied and served as a rabbi in Russia until he moved to the US in 1937. He was the leading halachic authority of American Jewry, and his responsa, which were widely circulated, are considered authoritative. Many of these responsa deal with modern technological problems.

Questions for Discussion

Compare and contrast these two cases:

1. How are these two cases similar? How are they different?

2. In which case does intervention seem more necessary from an ethical perspective? Why?

3. In view of the Jewish mandate to preserve life that we discussed in Lesson One, which of these cases seems more ethically problematic? Why?

The Elusive Definition of Life

Text 1

Henry Knowles Beecher (1904–1976) was an important figure in the history of anesthesiology and medicine, receiving awards and honors during his career. His 1966 *New England Journal of Medicine* article, on unethical practices in medical research, was instrumental in the implementation of federal rules on human experimentation and informed consent.

Only a very bold man, I think, would attempt to define death . . . . I was chairman of a recent ad hoc committee at Harvard composed of members of five faculties in the university who tried to define irreversible coma. We felt we could not define death. I suppose you will say that by implication we have defined it as brain death, but we do not make a point of that.

DR. HENRY K. BEECHER, QUOTED IN JEWISH BIO-ETHICS, P.278-9

The Right to Die

Text 2

At 2:47 a.m. on Dec. 26, 1990, twelve days after doctors in a Missouri state hospital removed her feeding tube, the life of 33-year-old Nancy Cruzan came to an end. For nearly eight years she had existed in a state of persistent vegetative coma, the result of injuries sustained when her car careened off a dark country road in rural southwestern Missouri. The decision to remove her from life support was made by her family and voiced by her father, Joe Cruzan. It was a wrenching choice, made only when all hope for recovery was extinguished. But the decision, it turns out, was only the beginning, for when the Cruzan family requested in May of 1987 that Nancy's life support be removed, doctors refused. And when, in 1990, her body was at last allowed to pass from life, the action was the culmination of a long and painful struggle, one that followed a path through the bastions of the U.S. legal system against fierce and powerful opposition, including Missouri Gov. John Ashcroft, and U.S. Solicitor General Kenneth Starr. Ultimately, the Cruzan case became the first "right-to-die" argument ever heard by the United States Supreme Court.

WILLIAM H. COLBY
LONG GOODBYE: THE DEATHS OF NANCY CRUZAN, JAN. 2003

Text 3

The watchword of the "death with dignity" movement is autonomy or self-determination. All well and good. What proponents of autonomy fail to realize, however, (or more ominously, what they realize and fail to express) is that as formerly unspeakable options become widely available, there is a tremendous societal pressure to have them exercised.

If and when assisted suicides become legalized and socially acceptable, one could easily visualize scenarios where persons who truly would want to live given the chance and the encouragement will instead opt for death, viewing their lives as worthless, nonproductive, and a drain on their families. Subtly or explicitly, societal consensus will push people into directions which on their own would have remained off-limits. What starts off as a *"right* to die" quickly turns into an *obligation.* Rather than enhancing autonomy and self-respect, the Derek Humphrey-Kevorkian approach does precisely the opposite, ultimately debasing the sanctity of the individual and the meaning of his existence. Judaism, which values and cherishes all life, inescapably proceeds from the opposite premise: . . . Life is regarded as a sacred trust given to us by G-d and only G-d can take it away.

As the great Talmudic sage Rabbi Chananya Ben Teradyon was being burned at the stake by the Romans for the "crime" of teaching Torah, and was suffering excruciating pain, his students urged him to open his mouth and let the flames enter so that he could die more quickly. He responded, "Let He who gave me life take it."

RABBI YITZCHOK BREITOWITZ
PHYSICIAN-ASSISTED SUICIDE: A HALACHIC APPROACH

Rabbi Dr. Yitzchok Breitowitz has published numerous articles on bankruptcy, commercial law, medical ethics, family law, and Halachah. In addition to being rabbi of the Woodside Synagogue in Silver Spring, Maryland, Rabbi Breitowitz is a professor of law at the University of Maryland.

The Value of Life

Text 4

Once we start making judgments as to which lives are worth living and which are not, once we assign value to people because of what they can *do* instead of what they *are* we have demeaned the intrinsic sanctity of existence for all human beings and have embarked on a dangerous exercise of line drawing. What about the elderly, what about the severely retarded, what about the handicapped: are they any less human because their productivity is impaired?

RABBI YITZCHOK BREITOWITZ
THE RIGHT TO DIE: A HALACHIC APPROACH

The Jewish Perspective on Sanctity of Life: Two Core Principles

Life Is Not Our Own

Text 5 ⚏

מצאוהו לרבי חנינא בן תרדיון שהיה יושב ועוסק בתורה
ומקהיל קהלות ברבים וספר תורה מונח לו בחיקו
הביאוהו וכרכוהו בספר תורה והקיפוהו בחבילי זמורות
והציתו בהן את האור והביאו ספוגין של צמר ושראום במים והניחום על לבו
כדי שלא תצא נשמתו מהרה
. . . אמרו לו תלמידיו: . . . אף אתה פתח פיך ותכנס בך האש
אמר להן: מוטב שיטלנה מי שנתנה ואל יחבל הוא בעצמו
אמר לו קלצטונירי: רבי, אם אני מרבה בשלהבת
ונוטל ספוגין של צמר מעל לבך, אתה מביאני לחיי העולם הבא?
אמר לו: הן. השבע לי! נשבע לו
מיד הרבה בשלהבת ונטל ספוגין של צמר מעל לבו
יצאה נשמתו במהרה

They took R. Chanina and wrapped a Torah scroll around him, and surrounded him with faggots of vine branches, to which they set fire. They brought woolen tufts, soaked them with water, and laid them on his heart, so that his soul should not depart quickly . . . . His disciples said to him: "Open your mouth that the fire may penetrate." He replied: "Better is it that He who gave the soul should take it, and that a man should do himself no injury." Then the executioner said to him: "Master, if I increase the flame and remove the woolen tufts from off thy heart, will you bring me to the life of the world-to-come?" "Yes," said Chanina. "Swear it," demanded the executioner. Chanina took the oath. The officer then increased the flame and removed the woolen tufts from over Chanina's heart, and his soul departed quickly.

Talmud, Avodah Zarah 18a

Every Moment of Life Is of Inestimable Value

Text 6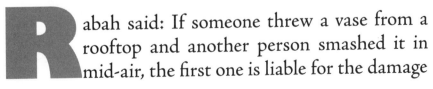

ואמר רבה: זרק כלי מראש הגג ובא אחר ושברו במקל, פטור

מאי טעמא? מנא תבירא תבר

ואמר רבה: זרק כלי מראש הגג והיו תחתיו כרים או כסתות

בא אחר וסלקן או קדם וסלקן, פטור

מאי טעמא? בעידנא דשדייה פסוקי מפסקי גיריה

ואמר רבה: זרק תינוק מראש הגג ובא אחר וקבלו בסייף

פלוגתא דרבי יהודה בן בתירא ורבנן

Rabah said: If someone threw a vase from a rooftop and another person smashed it in mid-air, the first one is liable for the damage and not the person who smashed it, for he had smashed a "broken" [doomed] vessel.

Rabah also said: If someone threw an infant from a rooftop and another person killed it with his sword in mid-air, [it is considered some form of murder, but] there is debate between R. Yehudah and the sages as to whether the person that actually killed [the infant] is subject to the death penalty.

TALMUD, BAVA KAMA 26B

Question for Discussion

Why is there a difference in ruling between the seemingly comparable cases of the vase and the infant?

Text 7 ▮

כל פיקוח נפש דוחה את השבת והזריז הרי זה משובח . . .
מי שנפלה עליו מפולת ספק עודנו חי ספק כבר מת . . .
מפקחין עליו אף על פי שיש בו כמה ספיקות שהרי אמרה תורה וחי בהם . . .
ואפילו מצאוהו מרוצץ שאינו יכול לחיות אלא לפי שעה
. . . מפקחים ומוציאים אותו בשביל חיי שעה

A danger to life suspends all the laws of the Sabbath, and the more a person acts with alacrity in this regard, the more praiseworthy that person is . . . . [For example] if a building collapsed on top of a person, even if there is a doubt whether he is alive or dead, or whether he is even under the rubble or not . . . one must dig through the rubble [to try and find him] . . . . For the Torah declares, "you shall live by them [the laws of the Torah] (Vayikra/Leviticus 18:5)" . . . . Even if one finds the person crushed, so that he cannot live for more than a short while, the rubble must be removed . . . . If there is any life in him at all, we remove him from the rubble, even for a few moments of life . . . .

RABBI SHNE'UR ZALMAN OF LIADI, SHULCHAN ARUCH HARAV (CODE OF JEWISH LAW), 329:1-4

Rabbi Shne'ur Zalman of Liadi (1745–1813), "the Alter Rebbe," author of *Tanya,* an early classic of Chassidism; *Torah Or; Likutei Torah;* and *Shulchan Aruch HaRav,* a halachic commentary. He founded the Chabad school of mysticism.

Text 8

רבי מאיר היה מושלו לנר שהוא מטפטף
כיון שנגע בו אדם מיד כיבהו
כך כל המעצם את עיני הגוסס
מעלין עליו כאילו הוא שומט את נשמתו

Rabbi Meir would say: This is compared to a flickering candle that is extinguished as soon as a person touches it. Likewise, whoever closes the eyes of a dying person is considered to have taken his soul.

TALMUD, SEMACHOT 1:4

A Chassidic Approach to the Quality of Life

Text 9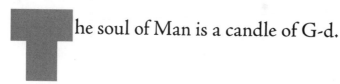

נֵר ה׳ נִשְׁמַת אָדָם

The soul of Man is a candle of G-d.

<small>M I S H L E I / P R O V E R B S 20:27</small>

Practical Applications

Text 10a

ההוא יומא דנח נפשיה דרבי, גזרו רבנן תעניתא ובעו רחמי
ואמרי: כל מאן דאמר נח נפשיה דרבי ידקר בחרב
סליקא אמתיה דרבי לאיגרא
אמרה: עליונים מבקשין את רבי והתחתונים מבקשין את רבי
יהי רצון שיכופו תחתונים את העליונים
כיון דחזאי כמה זימני דעייל לבית הכסא
וחלץ תפילין ומנח להו וקמצטער
אמרה: יהי רצון שיכופו עליונים את התחתונים
ולא הוו שתקי רבנן מלמיבעי רחמי
שקלה כוזא שדייא מאיגרא לארעא
אישתיקו מרחמי ונח נפשיה דרבי

On the day that Rabbi Yehudah HaNasi was to die the rabbis [his disciples] declared a fast and announced, "Let anyone who says that he has died be pierced with a sword."

The Rabbi's maidservant went up to the attic and prayed: "Those on high [angels] want our Rabbi and those below [the rabbis] also want our Rabbi. May it be Your will that those below overcome those above."

But when she saw that he was constantly going to the bathroom [he had a disease of the intestines—Rashi] and he had to remove his *tefilin* and then put them on again, which was causing him great pain, she said, "May it be Your will that those above overcome those below."

But when the rabbis did not cease begging for mercy for Rabbi Yehudah [so that his soul could not leave him] she took a clay vessel and threw it down from the attic to the ground. The rabbis stopped their prayers momentarily and his soul departed . . . .

TALMUD, KETUBOT, 104A

Text 10b

Rabeinu Nissim ben Reuven of Gerona (1320–1380) was considered the greatest halachic authority of his generation, and queries came to him from throughout the Diaspora. His works include commentaries on the Talmud and on Rabbi Yitzchak Alfasi's code, responsa, a commentary on the Bible, and a collection of sermons, *Derashot HaRan,* which elucidates fundamentals of Judaism.

נראה בעיני דהכי קאמר פעמים שצריך לבקש רחמים על החולה שימות כגון שמצטער החולה בחליו הרבה ואי אפשר לו שיחיה כדאמרינן בפרק הנושא (כתובות קד) דכיון דחזאי אמתיה דרבי

It seems to me that on occasion praying for compassion for a sick person [means praying] that he will die. For example, when the patient is in agony from his illness and cannot live, as stated in *Ketubot* in regard to Rabbi Yehudah HaNasi's maidservant . . . .

RABEINU NISSIM GERONDI
COMMENTARY ON TALMUD, NEDARIM 40A

Text 11

If the doctors do not know of a cure for the person's illness, nor of a means to reduce the person's pain, but merely know of a means to prolong his life of suffering, they should not apply these means . . . . If a person who is terminally ill contracts a second illness for which there is a cure, it is obligatory to heal him from the second illness . . . . However, if he is suffering, and there is no known cure [for the first illness], nor is there a means to relieve him of his pain and suffering, it is sometimes preferable for a person to die than to live under such circumstances . . . and it is probable that *we are not obligated to prolong his life.*

RABBI MOSHE FEINSTEIN, IGEROT MOSHE, CHOSHEN MISHPAT, VOL. 2, 74:1

Text 12

Since the suffering involving our case can be extremely difficult to tolerate, it would seem that one must have pity on the patient and reduce his suffering, especially in light of the fact that the suffering may cause to hasten his death even more than the pain medication . . . .

RABBI SHLOMO ZALMAN AUERBACH, ATERET SHLOMO, VOL. 7, P. III

Text 13

Not a single moment in a person's life is extra. Each person is given a particular number of days, hours and seconds for accomplishing his divine mission in life.

RABBI SHNE'UR ZALMAN OF LIADI, TORAH OR: MISHPATIM, P. 79

Key Points

1. What is often termed the "right to die" can quickly lead us down a slippery slope in which life is devalued and the sick and infirm are viewed primarily as burdens.

2. Judaism teaches that life is not our own, but rather, a sacred trust that we are obligated to protect.

3. Judaism also teaches that each moment of life is of inestimable value, the last moments no less significant than the first ones.

4. The very presence of life attests to a Creator, thus making the world a holy place.

5. G-d allots to each soul a certain span of life for completing its mission.

6. While we may not shorten life by even a moment, we are not obligated to undertake "heroic measures" to artificially prolong the life of a suffering person who is near death.

7. End-of-life issues are complex, and one should consult with a competent rabbi for guidance in making appropriate decisions in accordance with Jewish law.

Additional Readings

The Brain Death Controversy in Jewish Law

Rabbi Yitzchok A. Breitowitz

Historically, death was not particularly difficult to define from either a legal or *halachic* standpoint. Generally, all vital systems of the body-respiratory, neurological, and circulatory-would fail at the same time and none of these functions could be prolonged without the maintenance of the others. Today, with major technological advances in life support, particularly the development of respirators and heart-lung machines, it is entirely possible to keep some bodily systems 'functioning' long after others have ceased. Since we no longer face the inevitable simultaneity of systemic failures, it has become necessary to define with greater precision and specificity which physiological systems are indicators of life and which (if any) are not, especially in light of the scarcity of medical resources and the pressing need for organs for transplantation purposes. Over the past 20 or so years, the concept of "neurological death" commonly called "brain death," "whole brain death" or "brain stem death" (and, sometimes, inaccurately termed "cerebral death") has gained increasing acceptance within the medical profession and among the vast majority of state legislatures and courts in the United States. Whether this standard comports with *halacha* is a matter of great controversy among rabbinic authorities. The purpose of this article is not to take sides nor in any way resolve the *halachic* debate. Its purpose is more modest. This article will attempt to explain to the general reader: (1) what is "brain death" and how is it clinically determined; (2) some (not all) of the major sources on whether it is an acceptable criterion of death from the standpoint of *halacha*; (3) a "scorecard" on how contemporary authorities line up; and (4) the *halachic* and legal ramifications of one view or the other.

I. WHAT IS "BRAIN DEATH" AND HOW IS IT DIAGNOSED?

The concept of total "brain death" as an alternative to the older definition of irreversible circulatory-respiratory failure was first introduced in a 1968 report authored by a special committee of the Harvard Medical School[2] and was later adopted, with some modifications, by the President's Commission for the Study of Ethical Problems in Medicine and Biomedical Research, as a recommendation for state legislatures and courts.[3] The "brain death" standard was also employed in the model legislation known as the Uniform Determination of Death Act which has been enacted by a large number of jurisdictions and the standard has been endorsed by the influential American Bar Association. While New York is one of the few jurisdictions that does not have a "brain death" statute, it has adopted the identical rule through the binding decisions of its highest court.[4]

The rapid, and near universal, acceptance of neurological criteria of death is probably attributable to three factors. First, moving the time of death to an earlier point facilitates organ transplants, and indeed makes such transplants possible. Organs, especially hearts and livers, are suitable for transplantation only if they are removed at a time when blood is still circulating. Once cardiac arrest stops circulation, rapid tissue degeneration makes the organ unsuitable for such use. Given the increasing success of these operations and the relative uselessness (from a secular standpoint!) of sustaining "brain dead" patients on respirators, there is a natural temptation to redefine death so that organs become available to serve higher ends. It is no coincidence that the movement towards acceptance of "brain death" coincided with the development of cyclosporine and other anti-rejection drugs.

Additional considerations involve triage and allocation of scarce medical resources. It is extraordinarily expensive (in terms of equipment and labor) to maintain patients on respirators and other life support and using these resources for "brain dead" patients prevents their deployment for those who stand a better chance of recovery. Yet a third impetus towards redefinition is an understandable desire to spare families the agony and anguish of watching a loved one experience a protracted death.

For whatever the reason, the current definition of "death" is now a composite one: death is deemed to occur when there is either irreversible cessation of circulatory and respiratory functions (the "old" definition) or *irreversible cessation of all functions of the entire brain including the brain stem.*[5] The principal utility of this second standard permits declaring as dead a comatose, ventilator-dependent patient incapable of spontaneous respiration but whose heart is still beating due to the provision of oxygen via an artificial breathing apparatus.

At the outset, two points must be made absolutely clear. First, contrary to the misperceptions of many lay people, "brain death" is not synonymous with merely being comatose or unresponsive to stimuli. Indeed, even a flat EEG (electro-encephalogram) does not indicate brain stem destruction.[6] The human brain consists of three basic anatomic regions: (1) the cerebrum; (2) the cerebellum; and (3) the brain stem consisting of the midbrain, the pons, and the medulla, which extends downwards to become the spinal chord. The cerebrum controls memory, consciousness, and higher mental functioning. The cerebellum controls various muscle functions while the brain stem controls respiration and various reflexes (e.g., swallow and gag). A patient may be in a deep coma and nonresponsive to most external stimuli but still very much alive. At most, such patients may have a dysfunctional cerebrum but, by virtue of the brain stem remaining intact, are capable of spontaneous respiration and heartbeat. Indeed, the most famous of these cases, Karen Ann Quinlan, was able to live off a respirator for almost a decade. While such persons may be popularly referred to as brain dead, they are more accurately described as being in persistent vegetative state [PVS] and are very much alive under both secular and Jewish law. Removal of organs from such a donor would indisputably be homicide. This is even more true for the phenomenon known as being "locked-in" where the patient is fully conscious but unable to respond.

A second point to keep in mind is the relationship among respiration, circulation, and the brain. The heart, like any organ, or indeed cell, needs oxygen to survive and without oxygen will simply stop beating. Respiration, in turn, is controlled by the vagus nerve whose nucleus is located in the medulla of the brain stem. The primary stimulant for the operation of the nerve is the presence of excess carbon dioxide in the blood. When stimulated, the nerve causes the diaphragm and chest muscles to expand, allowing the lungs to fill with air. Spontaneous respiratory activity can therefore not continue once there is brain stem destruction or dysfunction. The heart, on the other hand, is not controlled by the brain but it is autonomous. It is obvious, of course, that the brain stem will inevitably lead to cardiac cessation not because of any direct control the brain stem exercises over the heart but simply because the heart muscle is deprived of oxygen. Where, however, the patient's intake of oxygen is being artificially maintained, the heart may continue to beat blood and circulate for a considerable amount of time after the total brain stem destruction. The time lag between brain death and circulatory death is on the average only two to ten days, though there is at least one case on record where a woman's heart continued to beat for 63 days after a diagnosis of brain death.[7] (Indeed, she delivered a live baby through Caesarean section.) It is this crucial gap between cessation of spontaneous respiration and cessation of the heart beat that defines the parameters of the phenomenon called "brain stem death."

The steps taken in a clinical diagnosis of "brain death" vary from medical center to medical center and those differences may have significant halachic repercussions but will typically involve the following:[8] (1) a determination that the patient is in a deep coma and is profoundly unresponsive to external stimuli; (2) absences of elicitable brain stem reflexes such as swallowing, gag, cough, sigh, hiccup, corneal, and vestibulo-ocular (ear); (3) absence of spontaneous respiration as determined by an apnea test;[9] and (4) performance of tests for evoked potentials testing the brain stem's responsiveness to a variety of external stimuli. These tests are to be repeated between 6-24 hours later to insure irreversibility—with life support supplied for the interim—and a specific cause for brain dysfunction must be identified before the patient will be declared dead.[10]

An additional test that is sometimes employed (when other clinical tests are deemed inconclusive) is radionuclide cerebral angiography [nuclide or radioisotope scanning]. A harmless radioactive dye is injected into the patient's bloodstream, typically through the intravenous tubing already in place. In brain dead patients, scanning will reveal an abrupt cutoff of circulation below the base of the brain with no visible fluid draining away. While many observers have described this test as nearly 100% accurate, others have claimed the brain stem circulation, especially in the medulla, is not well visualized and absolute absence of blood flow to this region cannot be diagnosed with certainty.[11]

Note that a patient who is brain dead may theoretically continue to have muscle spasms or twitchings or even sit up. Whether this so-called Lazarus Reflex is an indicator of life will be discussed in due course; what is undisputed is that such movements are coordinated not from the brain, but solely from the spinal cord. It should also be noted that there are several instances of clinically brain dead patients carrying live babies to term.[12] Again, this may or may not be significant.

II. IS BRAIN DEATH AN ACCEPTABLE HALACHIC CRITERION OF DEATH?

The question breaks down into distinct issues. First, is irreversible dysfunction of the entire brain a valid criterion of death? Second, even if the answer is yes, are the medical tests currently utilized in establishing such a condition halachically valid indicators of its presence? One could easily subscribe to "whole brain" death as a concept and yet reject the particular diagnostic tools employed.

There are a number of halachic sources that are relevant to the question of "brain death", the most important being the *Mishnah* in *Oholot* 1:6, the Talmud in *Yoma 85a*, passages in *Teshuvot Chatam Sofer* and *Teshuvot Chacham Tzvi*, and various pronouncement of R. Moshe Feinstein in his *Iggrot Moshe*.[13] This is not the forum for a detailed examination of these sources other than to note that a number of them are equivocal and subject to a variety of interpretations.

Briefly stated, the *Mishnah* in *Oholot* establishes the dual propositions that, first, physical decapitation of an animal is a conclusive indicator of death and second, some degree of subsequent movement is not incompatible with a finding of death provided that such movement qualifies as spastic in nature (*pirchis be'alma*) like the twitching of the "severed tail of a lizard." The Talmud in *Yoma 85a*, dealing with a person trapped under a building, rules that a determination of respiratory failure establishes death without the need to continue to uncover the debris to check heartbeat. Proponents of "brain death" argue that a dysfunctional brain stem is equivalent to a decapitated one (physiological decapitation), that destruction of the brain stem inevitably means inability to spontaneously respire (meeting the criterion in *Yoma*) and that subsequent "movement," whether the Lazarus Reflex or the heartbeat, falls into category of *pirchus* since such movement is not coordinated from a "central root and point of origin,"[14] i.e., the brain.

The counter-arguments are: first, physiological dysfunction is not the equivalent of anatomical decapitation. The only phenomenon short of actual decapitation that might similarly qualify is total liquefaction (lysis) of the brain, something that probably does not occur until well after cardiac arrest. Second, according to Rashi in *Yoma*, cessation of respiration is a conclusive indicator of death only when the person is "comparable to a dead man who does not move his limbs." While certain forms of postmortem movement may be characterized as merely spastic and would not qualify as "movement," the rhythmic coordinated beating of the heart and the maintenance of a circulatory system can hardly be characterized as *pirchus* since such a heartbeat is life-sustaining and identical to that in a normally functioning individual. Reference is also made to the *teshuvot* of *Chatam Sofer* and *Chacham Tzvi* who both write that it is only the cessation of respiration and pulse (heartbeat) that allows for a determination of death and the *Gemara* in *Yoma* merely creates a presumption that upon cessation of respiration and an appropriate waiting time, one is permitted to assume that heartbeat has stopped as well. Since this assumption is obviously not true in the case of "brain dead" patients hooked up to respirators whose heartbeats are monitored, such patients may not be declared as dead.

The position of R. Moshe Feinstein, whose psak could well have been definitive at least in the United States, is unfortunately a matter of some controversy. His son-in-law, Rabbi Dr. Moshe Tendler, a Rosh Yeshiva in RIETS and Professor of Biology, Yeshiva College, has vigorously argued the concept of decapitation in *Mishnah Oholot*.[15] His position finds strong support in *Iggrot Moshe*, *Yoreh De'ah III* no. 132 which seems to validate nuclide scanning as a valid determinant of death. This is also the understanding of the Israeli Chief Rabbinate, R. David Feinstein (who admits, however, to having no inside information on the topic), and R. Shabtai Rappaport, the editor of R. Moshe responsa.[16]

Others, however, have interpreted his *teshuvot* very differently, pointing out that R. Moshe reiterated twice (indeed, in one instance two years after the "nuclide scanning" reference) that removal of an organ for a transplantation was murder of the donor.[17] (R. Tendler's response: Both of those *teshuvot* refer to comatose patients in a persistent vegetative state who are capable of spontaneous respiration and are very much alive and not to those who are respirator dependent.) They also cite R. Moshe's express opposition to proposed "brain death" legislation in New York unless it contained a "religious exemption."[18] (R. Tendler's response: Although R. Moshe accepted the concept of "brain death," his support of an exemption was simply to accommodate the view of other religious Jews who disagree.) Finally, they note that in the very *teshuvah* upholding the use of angiographic scanning, R. Moshe approvingly cites *Teshuvot Chatam Sofer*, Y.D. no. 338, who insists on absence of *dofeik* to breathe, and no other sign of life is recognizable with them (*Vegam lo nikarim behem inynei chiyut achairim*). Their conclusion: R. Moshe merely validated nuclide scanning as a criterion to verify one determination of death, i.e., absence of respiration, but did not maintain that it alone was sufficient.[19] This author certainly lacks both the competence and the authority to resolve this dispute but presents it to the reader so that he may see why this area has been so fraught with unresolved controversy.

III. CONTEMPORARY VIEWS

The following is a cataloging of the major schools of thought among contemporary *poskim* and *rabanim* on the brain death issue and some of the recent events connected with this question.

1. As noted, Rabbi Dr. Moshe Tendler has been the most vigorous advocate for the halachic acceptability of brain death criteria. In his capacity as chairman of the RCA's Biomedical Ethics Committee, Rabbi Tendler spearheaded the preparation of a health-care proxy form that, among other innovations, would authorize the removal of vital organs from a respirator dependent, brain death patient for transplantation purposes. Although the form was approved by the RCA's central administration, its provisions on brain death were opposed by a majority of the RCA's own *Vaad Halacha* (Rabbis Rivkin, Schachter, Wagner and Willig).[20]

2. The Israeli Chief Rabbinate Council, in an order dated Cheshvan 5747, has also approved the utilization of "brain death" criteria in authorizing Hadassah Hospital to perform heart transplants but on a somewhat different theory than Rabbi Tendler. Positing that cessation of independent respiration was the only criterion of death (based on *Yoma* 85 but somewhat inexplicably also citing *Chatam Sofer*, Y.D. no. 338), the Rabbinate ruled that brain death was confirmatory of irreversible cessation of respiration. Theoretically, this would allow for a standard far less exacting than clinical brain death, perhaps nothing more than a failure of an apnea test. Indeed, Dr. Steinberg, the principal medical consultant to the Rabbinate, dismissed any requirement of nuclide scanning since destruction of the brain's respiratory center may be conclusively verified without such a test.[21] Since defining "death" exclusively in terms of inability to spontaneously respire would lead to the absurdity that even a fully conscious, functioning polio patient in an iron lung is dead, a subsequent communication from R. Shaul Yisraeli, a member of the Chief Rabbinate Council, qualified the Rabbinate's ruling by imposing, as an additional requirement, that the "patient be like a stone without movement"[22] (but apparently maintaining that heartbeat does not qualify as such movement). It is probable, though not certain, that R. Tendler's test of "physiological decapitation" and the Rabbinate's newly formulated test of "respiratory failure coupled with profound nonresponsiveness" amount to the same thing though the Rabbinate has not retracted from its non-insistence on nuclide scanning.

3. Rabbi J. David Bleich, Rosh Kollel at Yeshiva University and author of many papers and a recently published book on the subject, has stated that anything short of total liquefaction (lysis) of the brain cannot constitute the equivalent of decapitation. He further maintains, relying on Rashi in *Yoma*, the *Chatam Sofer*, and the *Chacham Tzvi*, that even total lysis would be insufficient in the presence of cardiac activity but dismissed the matter as being only of theoretical importance since cessation of heartbeat inevitably occurs prior to total lysis. He also asserts that his position is not based on stringency in case of doubt but rather on the certainty that the brain death patient is still alive, a certainty that could be relied upon even to be lenient, e.g., a Cohen may enter a "brain dead" patient's room without violating the prohibition of *tumat meit*.

4. Rabbi Aaron Soloveitchik, Rosh Yeshiva of Brisk and RIETS, has gone slightly further than Rabbi Bleich. Even if the heart has stopped and the patient is no longer breathing, the patient is alive if there is some detectable electrical activity in the brain.[23] It has been noted, however, that there is no recorded instance of this phenomenon occurring.

5. Rabbi Hershel Schachter, Rosh Yeshiva and Rosh Kollel of RIETS, has taken a more cautious view. Conceding that the concept of "brain death" may find support in the decisions of R. Moshe, he concludes that such a patient should be in the category of *safeik chai, safeik met* (doubtful life). While removal of organs would be prohibited as possible murder, one would also have to be stringent in treating the patients as *met*, e.g., a Cohen would not be allowed to enter the patient's room.[24]

6. Most contemporary *poskim* in Eretz Yisroel (other than the Chief Rabbinate) have unequivocally repudiated the concept of death based on neurological or respiratory criteria.[25] Of special significance are letters[26] signed by R. Shlomo Zalman Auerbach and R. Yosef Elyashiv, widely acknowledged as the leading *poskim* in Eretz Yisroel (if not the world), stating that removal of organs from a donor whose heart is beating and whose entire brain including the brain stem is not functioning at all is prohibited and involves the taking of life. Unfortunately, these very brief communications do not indicate if the *psak* is based on *vadei* (certainty) or *safeik* (doubt) nor do they address what the decision would be in case of total lysis.

IV. HALACHIC AND LEGAL RAMIFICATIONS

Obviously, in a matter so fraught with controversy, every family confronted with the tragic situation of a brain death patient must follow the ruling of its *posek*. To the extent the patient is halachically alive, removal of an organ even for *pikuach nefesh* would be tantamount to murder. The principle of *ain dochin nefesh mipnei nefesh*- that one life may not be set aside to ensure another life—applies with full force even where the life to be terminated is of short duration and seems to lack the meaning or purpose and even where the potential recipient has excellent chances for full recovery and long life. If, on the other hand, the

donor is dead, the harvesting of organs to save another life becomes a *mitzvah* of the highest order. In light of the overwhelming opposition to the "brain death" concept, caution and a stance of *shev v'al taaseh* (passivity) appears to be the most prudent course. How the "brain death" problem will play out in other areas such as inheritance, capacity of a wife to contract a new marriage, or the need for *chalitzah* if a man dies leaving a brain dead child will have to await further clarification.

There are, however, two other points that need to be considered. The argument is occasionally made if the *halachah* rejects the concept of "brain" or "respiratory" death, Orthodox Jews would be unable to receive harvested organs on the ground that the recipient would be an accessory to a murder. As others have noted,[27] this conclusion does not follow. To the extent the organ in question would have been removed for transplantation whether or not this specific recipient consents, i.e., there is a waiting list of several people, the Orthodox recipient is not considered to be a causative factor (*gorem*) in the termination of a life. There is no general principle in *halachah* that prohibits the use of objects obtained through sinful means. It is true that if, because of tissue typing and the like the organ is suitable for only one recipient and if that recipient declines the transplant, the organ will not be harvested, an Orthodox recipient may indeed be compelled to decline. But this is rarely, if ever, the case.[28]

A second point: as noted, "brain death" is the legal definition of death in the vast majority of the United States. New York is the only state that requires medical personnel to make a reasonable effort to notify family members before a determination of brain death and to make "reasonable accommodations" for the patient's religious beliefs.[29] In all other jurisdictions, doctors would be empowered unilaterally to disconnect a patient from life-support mechanisms once that patient meets a legal definition of death.[30] Hospital personnel may or may not defer to the wishes of the family but there is no duty on their part to do so or even to ascertain what those wishes are.[31]

Perhaps one point of consensus that may emerge in an area otherwise fraught with acrimonious controversy would be the desirability of enacting "religious accommodations" exceptions nationwide. After all, even the proponents of a "brain dead" standard understand that others, in all honesty and conscience, may hold a different *halachic* view, one which they should not be compelled to violate. Hopefully, our community will be responsive to such an effort.

V. CONCLUSION

"You preserve the soul within me and You will in the future take it from me " (Daily Prayers). Only God, Who is the source of all life, can take life away. We are enjoined to cherish and nurture life as long as it is present, no matter how fleeting or ephemeral. Yet it is precisely because each moment of life is so precious that God has imposed on man the awesome responsibility of defining the moment of death, the point after which the needs of the dead may, and indeed must, be subordinated to those of the currently living. No one has ever seen a *neshamah* leave a body and it is the unenviable task of our *gedolim* and *poskim* to tell us when this occurs. May *Hakodesh Baruch Hu* grant them the insight to truly make our Torah *Torat Chayim*.

Footnotes

1. The literature on brain death—medical, legal, halachic— is huge and only selective citations can be given here. The best *nonhalachic* survey of the legal and medical issues can be found in a report of the President's Commission for the Study of Ethical Problems in Medicine and Biomedical and Behaviorial Research, *Defining Death* (1981). Halachic treatment (as well as good discussion of related legal and medical approaches) can be found in a just-published book of Rabbi J. David Bleich, TIME OF DEATH IN JEWISH LAW (Z. Berman, 1991) which is a compendium of Bleich's previously-published Hebrew and English articles expounding his well-known opposition to "brain death" criteria. An excellent symposium (which also presents R. Tendler's opposing view) appears in Volume 17 of the JOURNAL OF HALACHA AND CONTEMPORARY SOCIETY (Spring 1989). Finally, the October 1991 JEWISH OBSERVER contains an interesting exchange of correspondence between Rabbi Tendler and Chaim Zweibel, General Counsel of Agudath Israel of America.

2. A Definition of Irreversible Coma—Report of the Ad Hoc Committee of the Harvard Medical School to Examine the Definition of Brain Death, 205 JAMA 337-350 (1968).

3. President's Commission for the Study of Ethical Problems in Medicine and Biomedical and Behavioral Research, Defining Death: Medical, Legal, and Ethical Issues in the Determination of Death (Government Printing Office, 1981).

4. See People v. Eulo, 63 N.Y. 2d 341 (1984).

5. Brain stem death occurs when, due to trauma, the brain swells and the pressure in the skull rises to exceed blood pressure. The brain is deprived of blood and oxygen and the brain tissue begins to liquify [lyse]. While total dysfunction occurs minutes after deprivation of oxygen, total liquification does not take place until some time after cardiac death, indeed sometimes several days after interment.

6. A good description of the scientific aspects of brain death can be found in 24 TRADITION 1, 8-14 (Summer 1989) (Dr. Jakobovitz's annotations to the Chief Rabbinate's ruling) and in Kielson, Determining the Time of Death-Medical Aspects, 17 JOURNAL OF HALACHA AND CONTEMPORARY SOCIETY 7-13 (Spring 1989).

7. See sources cited in Bleich, *Of Cerebral, Respiratory, and Cardiac Death*, 24 TRADITION 44, 61 n.5 (Spring 1989), reprinted in TIME OF DEATH IN JEWISH LAW, pp. 129-160.

8. Much of this information was derived from the articles cited in note 6 and a communication of Rabbi Moshe Tendler to the members of RCA dated Summer 1991.

9. Apnea testing takes many forms. One standard test may involve providing the patient with 100% oxygen for 20-30 minutes through the respirator and then shutting off the machine, thereby allowing the carbon dioxide in the blood to rise but at the same time allowing for passive gaseous diffusion of oxygen through the tubes of the machine or through a tube inserted directly into the trachea. This allows the CO_2 in the blood to rise, enabling a test of the respiratory response without depriving the patient of necessary oxygen in the interim. While a normally-functioning brain stem would induce respiration at a fairly low pressure of CO_2, a diagnosis of death will not be confirmed until the CO_2 pressure is considerably above the normal triggering point but nevertheless fails to elicit a respiratory response.

10. Note that a flat EEG (electroencephalogram) is not a necessary condition for a brain death diagnosis. A flat EEG does not in any event insure brain stem death but at best, indicates only absence of (perceptible) upper brain activity. Conversely, even in patients with a brain death diagnosis, sporadic, minimal EEG activity has occasionally been found. The Harvard criteria regard a flat EEG as helpful and confirmatory but not essential to a brain death diagnosis.

11. Compare letter of Rabbi Tendler printed in the October 1991 JEWISH OBSERVER with the degree of skepticism expressed by

Dr. Keilson, *supra* note 6, at 12. Indeed, some earlier studies had indicated that angiography only measures *deficit*, not cessation of blood flow even to the cerebrum and that up to 24% of normal blood flow could still be present. Modern refinements in these techniques probably allow for a definitive determination of zero blood flow to the cerebrum but "persistent perfusion and survival of the brain stem" remain a distinct possibility. See studies cited in Bleich, *supra* note 7, at notes 13-21. I have no information as to the accuracy of any of those studies; I simply point them out for the edification of the reader.

12. See the sources in the medical literature cited by Bleich, *supra* note 7 at 62 n.5 [at 133, n.5 in the book].

13. See *Teshuvot Chatam Sofer, Yoreh De'ah* no. 338; *Teshuvot Chacham Tzvi*, no. 77; and *Igrot Moshe, Yoreh De'ah* II, nos. 164, 174; *Yoreh De'ah* III, no. 132; *Choshen Mishpat* II, nos. 72-73.

14. See *Peirush HaMishnayot* of Rambam to *Oholot* 1:6.

15. See, for example, Rabbi Tendler's letter in October 1991 JEWISH OBSERVER.

16. The Chief Rabbinate's ruling accepting "brain death" explicitly relies on R. Moshe for authority. See TECHUMIM, Vol. 7, 187-192 (5746) and Jakobovits, *Brain Death and Heart Transplant: The Israeli Chief Rabbinate's Directives*, 24 TRADITION 1-14 (Summer 1989); R. David's understanding is quoted by R. Tendler in his own October letter to JO; and R. Shabtai Rappaport's letter appears in 12 ASSIA no. 3-4 (Kislev 5750), pp. 10-12.

17. See *Igrot Moshe, Yoreh De'ah* II, no. 174 (5728) and *Choshen Mishpat* II, no. 72 (5738). The *teshuva* in *Yoreh De'ah* III, no. 132 cited in support of brain death criteria was authored in 5736.

18. Written statement of 8 *Shevat* 5737.

19. It should be noted, however, that the *teshuva* concerning nuclide scanning was addressed to R. Tendler for his own guidance, surely entitling his understanding of the responsa to great weight.

20. The current status of the RCA proxy is unclear. In light of the negative psak of Rabbis Auerbach and Elyashiv, Rabbi Marc Angel, the President of the RCA., circulated a cover letter to the membership cautioning that the proxy form should not be used until the individual *rav* has thoroughly studied the issue and consulted experts in the field. Rabbi Tendler has similarly stated that at least portions of the proxy form were merely a "first draft" to be circulated to rabbanim. Yet the RCA continues to make the form available to the general public without informing them of these disclaimers. It is respectfully submitted that this inadvertent oversight be corrected.

21. Dr. Steinberg's paper, originally prepared to assist the Chief Rabbinate in their deliberations, appears in OR HAMIZRACH (Tishrai 5748).

22. Quoted in Bleich, TIME OF DEATH at 167-168.

23. His views may be found in 17 JOURNAL OF HALACHA at 41-50 (Spring 1989).

24. Rabbi Schachter's intermediate position may be found in the same journal at pp. 32-40.

25. These include R. Elazer Schach, Rosh Yeshiva of Ponevez; R. Yitzchok Weiss, recently deceased Rav of the Eida Chareidis; R. Yitzchak Kulitz, Chief Rabbi of Jerusalem; R. Eliezer Waldenberg, author of Tzitz Eliezer; R. Nisim Karelitz, Chief Rabbi of Ramat Aharon; R. Shmuel Wosner, late Rabbi of Zichron Meir; and R. Nosen Gestetner. References to those decisions can be found in Bleich, TIME OF DEATH at 144-145.

26. Letter of 18 Menachem Av 5751. A second letter reaffirming this stance was issued during the Aseret Yemei Teshuva 5752.

27. See comments of R. Soloveitchik, cited in note 22.

28. According to a just-published article in the JOURNAL OF THE AMERICAN MEDICAL ASSOCIATION (Jan. 1992), the demand for hearts, kidneys, and lungs far exceeds the available supply.

29. See 10 N.Y. C.R.R., sect. 400-16 (1987). The regulation mandating religious accommodation is also reprinted in an excellent article by Zweibel, *Accommodating Religious Objections to Brain Death: Legal Considerations*, 17 JOURNAL OF HALACHA 49 (Spring 1989).

30. Of course, even in New York, only "reasonable accommodation" is required and one can well imagine triage considerations forcing patients off respirators prematurely.

31. Moreover, even where doctors defer to the family's wishes, insurance companies may refuse to pay the costs of sustaining what is legally regarded as a cadaver. This is likely not to be a problem in New York since the regulatory duty of "reasonable accommodation" prevents a determination of brain death.

www.jlaw.com/Articles/brain.html

Reprinted with permission from JLaw.com

The Right to Die: A Halachic Approach

Rabbi Yitzchok Breitowitz

American society has increasingly come to recognize what is known as the "right-to-die". In the famous *Cruzan* case, the Supreme Court of the United States in a 5-4 decision ruled that a patient who has clearly communicated his or her wishes regarding the use of life support machinery or the provision of hydration and nutrition has a constitutional right to have those wishes respected *even if the patient is not suffering from a terminal condition*. Jack Kevorkian, the infamous doct or of death, is running around the country assisting persons in killing themselves. Derek Humphrey's work FINAL EXIT was a best seller. A referendum in the state of Washington that would formally legitimize physician-assisted suicides was supported by almost 50% of the electorate and many feel that within a few years, such measures will be routinely approved. Under a recently-enacted federal law, persons entering hospitals or nursing homes must be informed of their rights to execute living wills or other advance directives spelling out ahead of time that certain medical interventions should not be employed. What does the Jewish tradition say about these matters? Does *halacha* take positions on advance directives? Does Judaism recognize a right to die?

Briefly stated, the Jewish tradition rests on a number of assumptions:

1. The preservation of life [*pikuach nefesh*] is considered to be of paramount importance, surpassing virtually all of the other commandments of the Torah. One may *and must* violate Yom Kippur or the Sabbath, eat non-kosher food, *etc.* if there is the slightest chance that human life may be preserved or prolonged.

2. The quality and/or duration of the life being saved is irrelevant. Life is of infinite, not relative, value and mathematically, any fraction of infinity must also be infinite. Once life is assigned a relative value—once we start making judgments as to which lives are worth living and which are not, once we assign value to people because of what they can *do* instead of what they *are* we have demeaned the intrinsic sanctity of existence for all human beings and have embarked on a dangerous exercise of line drawing. What about the elderly, what about the severely retarded, what about the handicapped: are they any less human because their productivity is impaired?

[The reader may legitimately ask what use is the life of a Karen Ann Quinlan? What use is the life of a person who is comatose and incapable of any cognitive brain functioning? What use is an anencephalic child? Keep in mind, however, that a Jew believes in a soul and that the body is simply a receptacle for the person's true spiritual essence. Souls come to earth for many, many purposes and we don't know why G-d sends souls into this life. Sometimes it could be that the spiritual destiny of a soul is to elicit certain responses on our part. The soul exists to teach us certain things about the meaning of life and love and how we relate to the dignity of a human being and when we fail to respond with sensitivity and respect for the unconditional value of that person's life, we kill off a small part of ourselves as well.]

3. Judaism rejects the notion of unlimited personal autonomy. Our bodies and our lives are *not* our own to do with as we will. They are temporary bailments given to us by G-d for a specific purpose and duration which only G-d can terminate and just as we don't have the moral right to kill or harm others, we don't have the moral right to kill, maim, or injure ourselves or to authorize other persons to do those things to us.

4. Judaism rejects the notion that the utilization of advanced technology to sustain life is somehow an interference with G-d's will. Technology and scientific advancement are not man-made but are in themselves gifts of Divine revelation to be used for the benefit of mankind. Thus, the dichotomy that some religions posit between "natural" and "unnatural" ways of treating illness is essentially foreign to Jewish thinking.

These four factors standing alone would surely argue against any "right to die" and would support an absolute affirmative obligation to prolong life at all costs, regardless of pain and indeed regardless of the patient's expressed wishes. This is in the fact the position associated with the eminent Talmudist and bioethicist, Rabbi Dr. J. David Bleich of Yeshiva University. It is, however, a decidedly minority position.

Halacha, as all well-developed ethical systems, cannot and does not focus on a single moral value to the exclusion of others but seeks to balance, accommodate, and prioritize a multiplicity of ethical concerns. Just as there is a *mitzva* (a Divine commandment) to prolong life, there is a *mitzva* to alleviate pain and suffering. But what happens if one value can be achieved only at the expense of another? Consider the patient suffering terminal cancer whose life could be prolonged for no more than six months but only at the cost of painful, debilitating chemotherapy or the elderly stroke victim who falls prey to pneumonia which will kill him swiftly and relatively-painlessly overnight but is easily treatable by antibiotics. May the patient decline the chemotherapy or the antibiotics to achieve a quicker, less painful death or is the *mitzva* of *pikuach nefesh* (preservation of life) so absolute that it admits of no exceptions?

Most rabbinical authorities (Rabbi Moshe Feinstein, for one) have sanctioned the patient's right to decline treatment provided a number of very specific conditions were met. First, the patient must be in a terminal condition—that is, whether the treatment is employed or not, the patient is not expected to live beyond a year. Second, the patient suffers unbearable pain and suffering. Third, the patient has indicated that he or she desires not to be treated. In the event the patient is incompetent or unable to communicate his decision, next-of-kin may make such a decision based exclusively on what they feel the patient would have wanted (Note: This is not based on what *they* would have wanted if they would have been the patient but rather what this particular patient would actually desire). Fourth, assuming the above three conditions are met, the patient may decline surgery, chemotherapy, and painful invasive treatments but may not decline food, water, or oxygen (which are the normal sustainers of life, the withdrawal of which may be tantamount to murder or suicide). Antibiotics may also fall under the "food" category because they are generally a noninvasive, nonpainful procedure. There is also some question whether tube feeding falls in the category of "food" or in the category of "surgery". Most deciders would place it in the former but emphasize that even if the patient is *halachically*-obligated to take artificial nutrition, he should not be force-fed or physically-restrained. In no event may the patient or the physician take any affirmative step that would hasten death. Active euthanasia, regardless of motive, is morally and *halachically* equivalent to murder. On the other hand,

halacha would view both the goals and methods of hospice in a very sympathetic light.

Judaism thus attempts to strike a balance between the great *mitzva* of prolonging life and the recognition that life may become unbearably difficult and painful. The living will, however, which attempts to spell out in advance which treatments should be employed and which should not is too blunt of an instrument to accurately mirror the necessary value judgments. The basis for all of these decisions is the pain and suffering the patient feels at the time of the illness and this can simply not be predicted in advance. Conditions that may seem intolerable to us when we are 35-40 may be quite adequate when we reach 85 and we realize that the alternative would be death. Keep in mind too that many patients such as those with advanced Alzheimer's or in comas may in fact not be suffering though their existence is undoubtedly a hardship to their families. Moreover, it is almost impossible to spell out all contingencies in advance, making living wills incomplete almost by definition.

Far preferable to the living will is the durable power of attorney (often called a health-care proxy) which simply specifies a person—family member, friend, clergyman—empowered to make health care decisions on the patient's behalf in the event he or she is incapacitated. The power may in addition specify that all decisions shall be made in accordance with Jewish law and in consultation with a designated clergyman of the patient's choice. Sample forms—labelled somewhat inaccurately as "Halachic Living Wills"—have been prepared by Agudath Israel of America, a national organization headquartered in New York. This document insures that decisions will be made consistently with the moral and religious beliefs that the patient holds dear. Obviously, one should discuss these delicate matters ahead of time both with family members and spiritual advisers.

Incapacitation and terminal illness are tragic situations. Let us remember, however, that we come from a tradition that has grappled with these questions and that approaches these issues with sensitivity, compassion, and understanding. Hopefully, none of us will ever be faced with these problems but if we are, let us turn to our tradition for guidance and support.

Reprinted with permission from JLaw.com

End of Life Choices in Halacha

Daniel Eisenberg, MD

In many states, every patient admitted to a hospital must be offered the option of filling out "advanced directives," commonly known as a living will, indicating their medical wishes in case the patient is not competent to express their desires at a future time. A patient may also choose to execute a durable power of attorney, indicating to whom they would like to transfer legal authority to make medical decisions for them in case of incapacitation. While Judaism may not have encouraged the proliferation of living wills and durable powers of attorney, it has come to terms with them and recognizes the opportunity that these documents offer to have Jewish law applied in end of life situations. The most direct argument for advanced directives is the recognition that if the patient has not indicated his wishes in advance, someone else will and that person may not be someone whose choices the patient would accept.

Both the Agudath Israel and the Rabbinical Council of America have drafted model living wills and powers of attorney that are intended to meet the needs of the Torah-sensitive Jew. It is important to understand that advanced directives do not intrinsically require lack of treatment in cases of medical emergency. While one may legally choose to refuse life-sustaining treatment in cases of critical illness, one is also free to mandate that "everything" be tried. The Jewish person contemplating using a power of attorney may name their Rabbi to be their legal proxy, ensuring that any issues of Jewish law will be dealt with appropriately.

The crucial issue involved with a living will is whether the Torah grants the Jew the autonomy to refuse treatment. Rabbi Moshe Feinstein clearly allows the terminally ill patient in intractable pain to refuse life-prolonging treatment that will neither cure him, nor relieve his pain. Surely, such a patient may refuse resuscitation or intubation if he so chooses. A non-terminally ill patient may refuse treatment if the proposed therapy is sufficiently dangerous or unproven.

Regarding the durable power of attorney, we may gain insight from a different responsum. Rabbi Feinstein states that if a pain-stricken terminally ill patient were to develop a second illness for which there is a cure (such as a pneumonia in a terminal cancer patient), he may refuse treatment if he would prefer to die and it would be "proper not to treat him in any manner that would prolong the dying process", such as treating the second illness. Nevertheless, Rabbi Feinstein writes, this is a decision that the patient must make, and if the patient is incompetent, the doctor should consult the family regarding treatment, since they are closest to the patient. While the family's autonomy is limited by the same factors that limit the patient himself, we see that Judaism does recognize the concept of substituted judgment in such cases. A durable power of attorney is the easiest method of recognizing who should be consulted if the patient is incompetent.

The question of "do not resuscitate" orders is complex, yet fascinating. The Torah commandment of "do not stand by idly while your neighbor's blood is being spilled" (a mitzvah that is commonly understood to mean that everyone has a personal obligation to prevent his friend from being harmed) would seem to mandate compulsory resuscitation of everyone, since cardiac arrest and apnea certainly represent the ultimate in dangerous situations. Why then was it not always the custom to attempt CPR on every Jew who died?

The reason is because Judaism recognizes the inevitability of death. When someone dies, we are proscribed from desecrating the body, which includes invasion of the corpse. Moreover, the Code of Jewish Law (Shulchan Aruch) explains that there is a prohibition of touching a moribund patient (*goses*) who is estimated to have less than three days to live. Resuscitation of a *goses* is not required, and in fact may be prohibited, as a forbidden intrusion on the natural dying process. Therefore, the underlying assumption in Judaism is that one should NOT resuscitate a gravely ill patient, but only a patient for whom there is a reasonable expectation of reversing the underlying cause of physiologic collapse. As I mentioned in a previous article, one should not resuscitate a patient whose cessation of life functions is because their body could no longer sustain life. On the other hand, one must resuscitate a person whose physiologic collapse is secondary to a reversible illness, such as a treatable arrhythmia. Additionally, one may choose not to be resuscitated if the probability of success is low and the risk of painful disability is great. Therefore, in the right situation, a person may choose not to be resuscitated.

http://www.jlaw.com/Articles/EndofLife.html

Lesson 3
The Right to Life
Jewish Perspectives on the Beginning of Life

Introduction

The American public debate about abortion is often polarized between the pro-choice and pro-life positions. Yet most Americans tend toward a more moderate view. They want legal medical abortion available in cases of dire need, but are uncomfortable with the idea of abortion as a casual decision. Here are some statistics (taken from pro-abortion sources):

■ More than 1.3 million abortions are performed in the U.S. each year.

■ 10 percent of abortions occur after the first trimester.

■ 48 percent of abortions occur in women over the age of 25.

■ About 60 percent of abortions are obtained by women who have one or more children.

■ More than 50 percent of abortions occur in women with family incomes of over $30,000 per year; 14 percent of abortions occur in women with family incomes of over $60,000 per year.

■ An estimated 43 percent of all women will have had at least one abortion by the time they are 45 years old. 47 percent of all abortions are performed on women who have had at least one previous abortion.

■ 1 percent of all abortions occur because of rape or incest; 6 percent of abortions occur because of potential health problems regarding either the mother or child, and 93 percent of all abortions occur for social reasons (i.e., the child is unwanted or inconvenient).

What insights does Judaism shed upon abortion? How can we best balance the competing interests of mother and child?

Introduction:
Abortion in Jewish Law

Learning Activity 1

Consider the following hypothetical scenarios:

1. Dinah is expecting her third child when her husband suffers a massive stroke. It is uncertain if he will live, but even if he survives, the road to recovery will be arduous and the final outcome uncertain. Although she very much wanted this child before this tragedy struck, she has two other children to raise and a husband hovering between life and death. Carrying a baby to term seems too overwhelming. May she abort the fetus?

2. While Rachel is pregnant, it is discovered that she is harboring a malignant tumor that threatens to metastasize due to the hormones caused by pregnancy. If she carries the baby to term, it will likely be too late to treat her. May she abort the fetus?

Questions for Discussion

1. Would a radical proponent of the pro-life position see any difference between these two scenarios?

2. Would a radical proponent of the pro-choice position see any difference between these two scenarios?

3. How might you draw a relevant distinction between these two scenarios? In which case would you be more sympathetic to abortion, and why?

Text 1

האשה שהיא מקשה לילד מחתכין את הולד במעיה
ומוציאין אותו אברים אברים
מפני שחייה קודמין לחייו
יצא רובו אין נוגעין בו שאין דוחין נפש מפני נפש

If a woman in labor has a life-threatening difficulty, one dismembers the embryo within her, removing it limb by limb, for her life takes precedence over its life. But once its greater part (head) has emerged it may not be harmed, for we do not set aside one life for another.

MISHNAH, OHALOT, 7:6

Question for Discussion

Based on the principle outlined in Text 1, what would a Jewish court decide in the first case above? The second?

Learning Activity 2

Text 2

Ann, who suffered from bone marrow cancer, needed a transplant and found only one matching donor: her pregnant sister Leah. In order to perform the procedure without endangering Leah's life, an abortion was needed. Whose life takes precedence?

R. L.Y. HALPERIN, RESPONSA MA'ASEI CHOSHEV, VOL. 3, NO. 10

Question for Discussion

Using Text 1 as the basis for your argument, decide whether Leah should be allowed to abort her baby to save her sister Ann. Explain your reasoning.

When Does the Soul Enter the Body?

Text 3 📖

ואמר לו אנטונינוס לרבי:

נשמה מאימתי ניתנה באדם, משעת פקידה או משעת יצירה?

עומדת שלשה ימים בלא מלח ואינה מסרחת? אמר לו: משעת יצירה

אמר לו: אפשר חתיכה של בשר

אלא משעת פקידה

אמר רבי: דבר זה למדני אנטונינוס

ומקרא מסייעו, שנאמר "ופקדתך שמרה רוחי"

Antoninus . . . asked Rebbi: When is the soul placed into man? Is it from the moment of conception or from the moment of the embryo's formation [i.e., when it takes on human form]? Rebbi said: From the time of formation.

Antoninus said to him: Can a piece of meat remain for three days without salt and not become putrid? Must it not be, rather, that the soul enters the person from the moment of conception?

TALMUD, SANHEDRIN 91B

Text 4a 📜

דרש רבי שמלאי: למה הולד דומה במעי אמו?
לפנקס שמקופל ומונח
... ואוכל ממה שאמו אוכלת, ושותה ממה שאמו שותה
... ונר דלוק לו על ראשו וצופה ומביט מסוף העולם ועד סופו
... "שנאמר "בהלו נרו עלי ראשי לאורו אלך חשך
... ואין לך ימים שאדם שרוי בטובה יותר מאותן הימים
... ומלמדין אותו כל התורה כולה
וכיון שבא לאויר העולם, בא מלאך וסטרו על פיו
ומשכחו כל התורה כולה

abbi Simla'ei said: The fetus inside its mother's womb is like a folded document . . . . It eats from the mother's food and drinks from the mother's drink . . . . A light is lit over its head and it sees from one end of the world to the other, as it says: "His light shines upon my head" . . . . There are no better days for a person than the months spent in the womb. And they [the angels] teach it [the fetus] the entire Torah . . . . And as soon as it is about to emerge into the world, an angel comes and slaps it on the mouth, causing it to forget the entire Torah . . . .

TALMUD, NIDAH 30B

"A light is lit over its head and it sees from one end of the world to the other (Talmud, Nidah)." The light is a reference to the soul, as the soul is compared in the book of Proverbs to a candle of G-d. At the time when the fetus is in its mother's womb, it is not integrated with the body. It achieves a total union with the body upon its emergence into the world . . . . This is the meaning of "a light is lit over its head"—even though the soul is already present in the body, it is not totally integrated with it. It is merely "over its head."

RABBI YEHUDAH LOEW (MAHARAL)
CHIDUSHEI AGADOT ON TALMUD, NIDAH

Rabbi Yehudah Loew of Prague (1525–1609), "The *Maharal*," thinker and mystic. Author of *Gevurat HaShem*. Thousands visit his resting place in the old Jewish cemetery of Prague.

Two Basic Positions About Abortion: Rashi and Rambam

Text 5a

האשה שהיא מקשה לילד מחתכין את הולד במעיה
ומוציאין אותו אברים אברים
מפני שחייה קודמין לחייו
יצא רובו אין נוגעין בו שאין דוחין נפש מפני נפש

If a woman in labor has a life-threatening difficulty, one dismembers the embryo within her, removing it limb by limb, for her life takes precedence over its life. But once its greater part (head) has emerged it may not be harmed, for we do not set aside one life for another.

MISHNAH, OHALOT, 7:6

Text 5b

Rashi (Rabbi Shlomo Ben Yitzchak) (1040-1105) of France, considered one of the greatest Jewish scholars of all time. His authoritative commentary on the Talmud is included in all printed versions of the Talmud.

דכל זמן שלא יצא לאויר העולם לאו נפש הוא

The reason is that a fetus is not a *"nefesh"* (a full living soul).

RASHI, COMMENTARY ON TALMUD SANHEDRIN 73B

הרי זו מצות לא תעשה שלא לחוס על נפש הרודף
לפיכך הורו חכמים שהעוברה שהיא מקשה לילד
מותר לחתוך העובר במיעיה בין בסם בין ביד
מפני שהוא כרודף אחריה להורגה
ואם משהוציא ראשו אין נוגעין בו שאין דוחין נפש מפני נפש
וזהו טבעו של עולם

This too is a negative commandment: not to have compassion on the life of a pursuer. Therefore, the sages ruled that when a woman has difficulty in labor, one may dismember the embryo within her, either with drugs or surgery, because it is like a pursuer seeking to kill her. But once the head has emerged, he may not be harmed, for we do not set aside one life for another. This is the natural course of the world.

RAMBAM, MISHNEH TORAH, HILCHOT ROTZEACH (LAWS OF MURDER) 1:9

R. Moshe ben Maimon (1135–1204), better known as Maimonides or Rambam, author of *Mishneh Torah*, a compendium of Jewish law, and *Guide for the Perplexed*. He was born in Córdoba, Spain. After the conquest of Córdoba by the Almohads, who sought to forcibly convert the Jews to Islam, he fled and eventually settled in Cairo. There he became the leader of the Jewish community and served as court physician to the vizier of Egypt.

Question for Discussion

Who would be more inclined to allow Leah to abort her fetus to save her sister Ann: a rabbi following the reading of Rashi, or one following the reading of Maimonides?

Text 6 ▮

אמר רב נחמן אמר שמואל: האשה שישבה על המשבר ומתה בשבת
מביאין סכין ומקרעים את כריסה ומוציאין את הוולד . . .
להביא סכין דרך רשות הרבים

Said R. Nachman in the name of Shmuel: When a woman dies on the Sabbath while she is on the birth stool, one brings a knife to cut open her abdomen and remove [i.e., save] the fetus . . . even if he must carry the knife by way of the public domain.

TALMUD, ARACHIN, 7A

Question for Discussion

Does this support Rashi's position or Rambam's position?

Text 7 ▮

עוברה שהריחה מאכילין אותה עד שתשיב נפשה

If a pregnant woman . . . smelled food on Yom Kippur and developed a craving for that food, one must feed her until she regains her senses.

TALMUD, YOMA 82A

Question for Discussion

Does this text support Rashi's position or Rambam's position?

Text 8a

וְכִי יִנָּצוּ אֲנָשִׁים וְנָגְפוּ אִשָּׁה הָרָה וְיָצְאוּ יְלָדֶיהָ וְלֹא יִהְיֶה אָסוֹן
עָנוֹשׁ יֵעָנֵשׁ כַּאֲשֶׁר יָשִׁית עָלָיו בַּעַל הָאִשָּׁה וְנָתַן בִּפְלִלִים
וְאִם אָסוֹן יִהְיֶה וְנָתַתָּה נֶפֶשׁ תַּחַת נָפֶשׁ

If men strive together and hurt a woman with child, so that her fruit depart and yet no harm follows, he shall surely be fined . . . and pay as the judges determine. But if any harm follows, you shall give a life for life [i.e., capital punishment].

SHEMOT/EXODUS 21:22-23

Text 8b

"ולא יהיה אסון" –באשה
"ענוש יענש" –בולדות

"Yet no harm follows" refers to harm to the woman. "He shall surely be fined" refers to compensation for the loss of the fetus.

MECHILTA (MIDRASH ON SHEMOT), MISHPATIM

Question for Discussion

Does this support Rashi's position or Rambam's position?

Contemporary Applications
When It Is Unclear That the Baby Is a *Rodef*

Learning **Activity 3**

Text **9**

A woman is bleeding profusely during pregnancy. Her life is in danger. The doctor determines that in order to attempt a procedure which might stop the bleeding, the fetus must be removed. However, the doctor is not certain whether the condition is caused by the pregnancy or whether it is an independent condition rendered more difficult to treat because of the presence of the fetus. Thus, the removal of the fetus might or might not help her condition. May one remove the fetus on the possibility that it may save her life?

RABBI YITZCHOK SHOR, KO'ACH SHOR, NO. 20

Question for Discussion

What implications does Rashi's view have for this case? What implications does Rambam's view have for this case?

Key Points

1. The question of abortion is not one of rights, but of obligations.

2. The relationship between soul and body is both revolutionary—reflecting a dramatic change from lifeless to alive, and evolutionary—as the child develops over time. Life begins at conception, though it continues to unfold over the duration of the gestational period.

3. Human life—even potential life—is sacred, and terminating it is a very serious act that can only be contemplated in the direst of circumstances.

4. There are two main schools of thought on abortion in Jewish thought, which can be traced to Rashi and the Rambam.

5. According to Rashi, the fetus is not yet considered a full living soul, and although termination of the pregnancy is forbidden as mutilation of the body, it is permissible in cases with overriding justification, such as threat to the mother's life and health.

6. According to the Rambam, the fetus is a living soul whose life can only be terminated when it threatens the life of the mother, as outlined by the laws of *rodef.*

7. Although many sources seem to support one or the other position, in fact they can be read to support either. Most contemporary authorities follow Maimonides, although at least one important arbiter follows Rashi; this may affect the degree of difficulty required for dispensation to abort.

Additional Readings

How A Rabbi Decides A Medical Halacha Issue

Synopsis of Presentation
Conference on Jewish Medical Ethics
San Francisco, CA
February 18-20, 1996

Rabbi Yitzchok A. Breitowitz

I. Secular law is primarily concerned with *who* gets to make a decision. Courts and legislatures are thus preoccupied with advance directives, surrogate decision-making, ethics committee, IRBs *etc*. This is so because the primary value the law seeks to enshrine is the *autonomy* of the individual. Thus, once we identify the "who", we essentially have no interest in the "what". By contrast, Jewish law is far more interested in the substance of what the decision should be and in theory, the resolution should not depend on the identity/personal predilections of the decider. Secular law asks *who* decides; Jewish law asks *what is to be decided*.

II. *Limited Role of Autonomy in Jewish Law*

A. My body is not my own; it is the property of G-d who has entrusted it to me for care and preservation. Thus, the premise of the pro-choice movement (we have absolute control over our bodies) is fundamentally flawed (even apart from the fact that abortion involves a fetus as well as a mother). There is even discussion in *halachic* literature concerning the permissibility of elective cosmetic surgery both in terms of the surgical risks and in terms of the "mutilation" of G-d's property. (By and large, however, it has been validated).

B. R. Shlomo Yosef Zevin wrote a classic article demonstrating that in the *Merchant of Venice*, Antonio's contract with Shylock to pay a pound of flesh in the event of a loan default is unenforceable under Jewish law. Just as Antonio cannot pledge assets that he doesn't own, he cannot create such a pledge on his body.

III. *Limited Role of Charisma/Inspiration*

Halachic decision-making is not a matter of a Rabbi secluding himself in a room and getting a direct answer from G-d which he then communicates with *ex cathedra* authority. Indeed, based on the verse, "It [the Torah] is not in Heaven", the Talmud declares that prophecy and Divine inspiration *cannot* be taken into account in the resolution of *halachic* questions. *All halachic* resolution depends on a solid empirical grounding in the facts coupled with a *reasoned* application from the primary texts that Jewish law considers to be definitive, *e.g.* Talmud, Codes. *Ad hoc* decision-making that is not rooted in these texts is generally illegitimate.

IV. *Written Torah/Oral Torah*

Although the Pentateuch is the highest source of law in Judaism, the meaning of that written Torah can be understood only by means of the simultaneous oral interpretation that was handed down with it (the Torah She'Bal Pe). In its essence, the Torah She'Bal Pe was a core of principles and interpretations. Like a snowball, the core which originated in Divine revelation grew larger and larger as each generation had to apply these core principles to new situations, applications which sometimes generated disagreement (*machloket*). Although the core principles were part of a received tradition, the specific applications were the function of the Torah leadership/halachic authorities in each community to apply.

This growing "snowball" or avalanche was preserved orally for hundreds of years. Indeed, Jewish law *forbade* the writing down of the oral law, perhaps to insure that the meaning of the tradition would be communicated through flesh and blood human interaction, rather than exclusively through a literary medium. (It should be noted that many cultures—Native American, ancient Greece—preserved huge amounts of data through oral transmission for hundreds of years.) Only when (as a result of Roman persecutions in the first and second centuries of the common era) the oral law was in grave danger of being forgotten was it reduced to some type of written form as the Mishna. Several hundreds of years of commentary on the Mishna eventually formed the work known as Gemara. (There is both a Babylonian and

Palestinian Gemara though the Babylonian is regarded as the more authoritative.) Mishna and Gemara together form the work known as Talmud, second in importance only to the Pentateuch but whose influence on Jewish law has even been greater.

V. *Talmud: Source of Principles of Jewish Law*

The Talmud, particularly the much larger portion known as Gemara, is *not* a code of law; it rarely provides definitive *halachic* rules. It is rather a transcript of hundreds of years of debates espousing a multiplicity of positions. It illuminates the *process* and *conceptual structure* of *halacha* through reasoned analysis, logic, analogy, and proof-text but does not indicate a final rule. All *halachic* decision-making, however, is ultimately grounded in Talmudic conceptualization. The classic and definitive codifications of Judaism—Rambam's *Mishna Torah*, Tur, and *Shulchan Aruch* are all based on conclusions derived from the Talmudic *sugyot* (treatments). The responsa literature—a vast body comprising thousands of volumes from every part of the world—attempts to apply Talmudic discussions and the rulings of the codes to contemporary situations, thereby insuring that *halacha* remains a living, vital tradition.

VI. *Halachic Reasoning: Combination of Inductive and Deductive Logic*

Halachic reasoning, in common with all reasoning by analogy, involves a combination of inductive and deductive logic. First, *relevant primary data*—rulings in particular cases extracted from Talmud and Codes—*have to be identified and collected*. Second, *through inductive reasoning*, a hypothesis is formulated that explains the specific collection of rulings by reference to a more general principle. Third, *through deductive reasoning*, this principle can be utilized to apply to new situations that are not explicitly covered by the earlier rulings but can now be subsumed under the principle that is believed to explain those earlier rulings. Uncertainty, ambiguity, and disagreement among *halachic* scholars can arise at any stage of this three-stage process.

Identification of Primary Data: Widely scattered, not centrally located, no real indexing. Especially in the case of Talmud, concepts that are highly relevant in one area,

e.g., laws of Shabbat, may be discussed extensively in an apparently unrelated area, *e.g.*, marriage. Moreover, various rulings or conclusions that appear to be stated as definitive in the course of a discussion may not survive the conclusion of a debate though the Talmudic text does not always make this point clear. Moreover, even conclusions that appear to be "final" may be contradicted, superseded, or modified by other *sugyot* or subjected to limitations or conditions not apparent from a particular discussion but derivable by implication from another Talmudic source.

Even after the primary data and rulings have been identified, there remains the problem of interpretation—what does Rule X say? What does Rule X mean? There may be sharp disagreements among commentators and codes.

Generalization: As is true in physical science, data may offer a variety of hypotheses and the plausibility of a given explanation may give way to multiple views.

Application: Finally, the third stage which involves the application of the generalized principle to new cases may pose difficulties in determining whether or not the "new case" fits the parameters enunciated by the principle. This may require a reexamination or reformulation of what the generalization really encompasses as well as a careful understanding of the factual aspects of the "new case" to determine whether it is embraced by the paradigm.

"Cheating": Not every rabbi engages in this process for every question. In daily practice, we do not always reinvent the wheel and will often rely on the decisions of the great *poskim* of our day. Nevertheless, even if in practice most rabbis simply "follow the authorities", someone—*e.g.*, R. Moshe, must go through all the steps of the process.

VII. *The Crucial Importance of Knowing and Understanding the Facts on the Ground*:

Even if the rabbi has full mastery of the *halachic* sources, his decisions are likely to be incorrect unless he fully understands the medical background of the case. Garbage in = Garbage out. See Dr. Keilson's article reproduced in the loose-leaf that rabbis may be characterized along the lines of the Four Sons of the Pesach Hagada:

(1) *Wise*—the one who knows how to ask the proper questions and evaluate the response.

(2) *Evil* (or incompetent)—fairly rare, the one without the *halachic* expertise to render a valid decision.

(3) *Simple*—a rabbi who doesn't really understand the issue in a case.

(4) *One Who Doesn't Even Ask*—a rabbi even if learned who rules without even consulting with the physicians as to what the medical facts are.

VIII. *The "Art"/Judgment of Proper Pigeonholing*: The critical importance of defining the question so that the appropriate analogies will be drawn. If an external phenomenon is perceived or described in a certain way, then one set of *halachic* categories and constructs will be brought to bear. If the situation is perceived differently, other *halachic* concepts may become relevant. The process of "shaping" or identifying the critical and significant components of the phenomenon is often the most crucial step in being able to resolve the *halachic* quandary properly. Thus, "*sheealat chacham chatzi teshuvah*"—"the question of a wise man is half the answer."

IX. *The Role of Subjectivity in Psak*

In theory, *psak halacha* should not be subjective but is to be predicated exclusively on the *posek's* objective understanding of the principles of Jewish law as derived from its authoritative sources. In cases, however, of genuine unresolved disagreement (some authorities conclude one way, others conclude another way), the *halachic* system does contain within its own structure the recognition of extenuating circumstances that may allow the consideration of particular "extralegal" factors in a case. These include, in part, concepts such as "hefsed merubah" (great financial loss), "shaat ha'dechak" (a situation of urgency), "shalom bayit" (promotion of domestic tranquility in a marriage), "darchai noam" (the ways of the Torah are ways of pleasantness, not dissention). It must be emphasized that these factors alone are rarely taken into account in determining *halacha* on a primary level. In the event that the objective *halachic* considerations are balanced in both directions, however, these subjective factors will often tip the scale.

(I should also note that some *subjective* conditions become *objectively* significant even on the primary level. For example, abortion is *halachically* permitted if the continuation of the pregnancy endangers the mother's life. This endangerment may very well include severe psychiatric trauma which carries a suicide risk. Whether or not a given event, *e.g.*, rape or incest, creates such a risk depends entirely on the subjective mental state of the women. Obviously, the Rabbi cannot answer such a question with his nose buried in the books, but must be sensitive to the individual characteristics of the questioner.)

X. *Hearing the Question Not Asked*

The burden of identifying the question and ferreting out the information does *not* rest on the questioner who after all may be ignorant of what Jewish law regards as significant. Moreover, it is not enough to simply answer the precise question asked—the rabbi must have the sensitivity to address the "questions behind the questions"—concerns that might be implicit in the question asked but which were not explicitly articulated by the questioner. Thus, the rabbi must be more than the equivalent of an on-line database.

Story: A woman once asked the *Bais Ha'Levi* (the Rav of Brisk; great-grandfather and namesake of Rabbi Joseph B. Soloveitchik of Boston) whether one could fulfill the obligation of the Four Cups at the Seder with milk? The *Bais HaLevi* answered in the negative and immediately gave the woman funds to buy meals for all of Passover. His disciples asked him why he didn't just give her enough money for wine. His answer—the last two cups of the *seder* are drunk *after* the meal. If the woman plans to use milk for the *last* two cups, it could only be because she has neither meat nor chicken to serve at the Seder meal. If there is no meat or chicken for the Seder—usually the most festive Pesach event—there is obviously none for the rest of the holiday. She accordingly needs funds for the entire holiday. The duty of the rabbi is to address the *entire* problem or more accurately, the whole person—not merely the segment of the problem that is explicitly raised.

Lesson: A rabbi answers a *questioner*—not a *question*.

XI. *The Individualized Nature of Psak Halacha*

R. Yitzchok Hutner, a renowned Rosh Yeshiva, once told a disciple: "Do not rely on *anything* that I ever said to someone else. Each *psak* is unique."

See also the comments of R. Moshe Feinstein in the introduction to his first volume of responsa (Igrot Moshe Orach Chayim I) where he writes that his responsa represent suggested approaches and general guidelines with each *rav* using his own judgment and discretion in applying the responsa to the facts of his particular case. Moreover, R. Moshe argues that each *rav* bears the responsibility of analyzing the primary sources on his own rather than blindly accept R. Moshe's reading of them.

Note: These warnings are commonly disregarded in practice. We often "cheat" and apply R. Moshe's rulings mechanically without analysis of the sources, without full knowledge of all the circumstances of R. Moshe's own *psak* (some of which may not always be stated) and without full consideration of all of the unique circumstances of the case upon which the rabbi is called to rule.

XII. *The Importance of Empathy and Respect for the Feelings of the Questioner Even Where Consideration of Such Feelings Has No Direct Impact on Halachic Resolution.* (This is equally true for physicians as well.)

XIII. *Pluralism and Mutual Respect in Halacha*

Unlike mathematic truth where there can only be one "true" answer (1 + 1 can *only* be two—but even here, there may be multiple answers in non-Euclidean systems), *halachic* truths can be multiple. Thus, the Talmud states concerning the opposing and inconsistent views of Bait Hillel and Bait Shammai: *"Elu V'Elu Divrei Elokim Chayim"*. "These and those are words of the Eternal G-d". This is so because ultimate truth is not a point but a process—as long as there is commitment to the theological postulates of the system (*e.g.*, the Divine origin of the Torah) and to the accepted *halachic* methodology and use of authoritative texts, *any* conclusion that the conscientious rabbi arrives at will have the imprimatur of valid *psak* even if in some sense it is not quite "what G-d may have intended."

Story: The Talmud relates that R. Eliezer disputed the view of the Sages concerning the ritual impurity of an oven. Refusing to concede his position, he declared: "If the law is like me, let the carob tree uproot itself." The tree did but the Sages declared, "We don't listen to trees." He then continued, "If the *halacha* is like me, let the river reverse its course." It did but the Sages stated, "we don't listen to rivers." He then said, "If the *halacha* is like me, let the walls of the study hall collapse " The walls were about to collapse but R. Yehoshua ordered them to remain. Uncertain how to proceed, the walls remained in a slanted position. Finally, R. Eliezer called out the big guns: the support that had in fact been the basis for the three miracles, G-d Himself. G-d declared, "R. Eliezer is correct." Amazingly, the Sages refused to accept even the direct opinion of G-d and declared, "Lo BaShamayim He"—the Torah is no longer in heaven. It was given to human beings to interpret and apply to the best of their abilities; prophecy, charisma, miracles are not determinative and even if a given *halachic* decision may be in error, it is validated by adherence to the process which the Torah itself sets up. When there is a supreme body like the 70-member Sanhedrin, their decision (by a majority) would be binding and preclusive on the minority dissenters but in the absence of such an authoritative body (as is the case today), there can indeed be multiple *halachic* approaches to many questions with none of them being "wrong" or "illegitimate". (Note, however, that I am not suggesting infinite flexibility—there are clearly standards and parameters that are absolute but as is obvious to any student of *halacha*, within the framework there is room for play at the joints.)

XIV. The obligation to develop a relationship with a rav on a permanent rather than *ad hoc* basis: "Aseh l'cha Rav"—"make for yourself a teacher." (Pirkei Avot).

A. Rav should be knowledgeable in particular area—whether medicine, business, etc.

B. Know *you* as a person to be able to take account of individual circumstances.

C. Improper to "shop around"—looking for the *rav* who will always give you the answer you want. However, with respect to *categories* of questions, it is legitimate to have one authority you turn to for medical issues and one for *kashrut* or marriage counseling if you feel that one rav is less qualified in a particular area. I reiterate, however, this should not be done simply because you like one rabbi's answers more. Rather your decision, should be based on general considerations of competence, judgment, and experience.

D. A good *rav* like a good doctor knows when to refer to greater authorities or to non-rabbinic experts, *e.g.*, therapists, psychiatrists and the like.

APPENDIX

Valuable Halachic Sources in Medical Halacha (very partial)

Dr. Abraham, *Nishmat Avraham* (4 Volume)

Assia (Israeli journal on medical halacha—ed. by Dr. Steinberg)

Bar-Ilan Computerized Responsa Project—hundreds of volumes of responsa on CD-Rom with search capacities; full text retrievals; in Hebrew only

Rabbi Bleich, *Contemporary Halachic Problems* (4 volumes to date)

Rabbi Bleich, *Judaism and Healing*

Nehorai—Specialized computer data base for medical *halacha*; special strength is its list of search terms.

Dr. Rosner, *Modern Medicine and Jewish Law*

Dr. Steinberg, *Encyclopedia L'Hilchot Refuah* (5 volumes to date)

http://www.jlaw.com/Articles/decide.html

Reprinted with permission from JLaw.com

Lesson 4
Words That Wound

Slander, Free Speech, and the Protection of Privacy

Introduction

n our first encounter with G-d in the book of Genesis, we see G-d as the Creator of heaven and earth. This monumental event is described as an act of speech: "And G-d said, 'Let there be light." The Kabbalah tells us that G-d's speech continues to sustain all of existence.

Human speech, of course, does not create worlds from nothingness, nor render them back into naught. Yet speech is the faculty that most sharply differentiates us from other living creatures, and it is the most powerful tool that we wield. Indeed, Solomon, wisest of all men, stated that life and death are in the hand of the tongue . . . .

Overview of Harmful Speech

Case Study 1

In 1994, Motty Lerner, an Israeli movie producer, produced a television show called "Kastner". The show was based on the famous story of Dr. Rudolph Kastner, a Zionist leader in Nazi-occupied Hungary in 1944, who was later charged before an Israeli court for the crime of collaborating with the Nazis.

The Nazis had learned, from the experience of the Warsaw Ghetto's uprising, that it was important to secure the help of the Jewish leadership in order to hide the true purpose of the train journey to Auschwitz, to make sure there would be no organized resistance. According to the evidence presented to the Israeli courts, Eichman struck a deal with Kastner, in which Eichman agreed to allow the rescue of some Jews from Hungary, and in return Kastner ensured that the 800,000 Jews of Hungary would be calm and cooperative while the Nazis deported them to Auschwitz. Kastner, who was trusted by the Jews, convinced them that they were being taken to a peaceful town where they would stay on farms until the war was over. In return, Kastner handpicked 600 Jews (most of whom were friends and relatives) to be transported to safety.

Kastner was also accused of bringing about the execution of Chana Senesh by the Nazis, as well as delivering two agents of the Jewish Agency, Palgi and Goldstein, to the Nazis. Chana Senesh was one of three brave members of the Jewish Agency in Palestine who parachuted into Hungary during its Nazi occupation, to warn the Jews of Hungary about the impending danger and to help them attempt to escape. Chana Senesh was caught very soon after she landed. She was tortured in order to extract information from her about the other two members of the Jewish Agency who were hiding at the time. She bravely endured the horrible torture without disclosing any information about her colleagues. She was executed shortly after.

Chana Senesh became a national heroine in Israel. She is seen as a symbol of Jewish sacrifice and courage. However, the show, which was written in honor of the fiftieth anniversary of Senesh's death, contained a line in which Kastner told Chana Senesh's mother in court, during her testimony against him, that it was Senesh who broke under torture and delivered the information about Palgi's and Goldstein's whereabouts to the Nazis. (In fact, Kastner never said any such thing.) Senesh's family and friends sued to prevent its airing because they saw this false line as slanderous and offensive to the honor of Chana Senesh. Many national organizations agreed.

The question around which this case revolved is whether one should restrict artistic freedom in light of the possible dishonor to an individual. Motty Lerner did not pretend to make a factual statement about who betrayed the two Israeli agents. He inserted this line purely for its dramatic effect. Did he have the right to artistic expression despite the shadow it cast over the memory of Chana Senesh?

Questions for Discussion

1. Does Lerner have the right to malign Senesh? Does it make a difference that it is in the context of a play?

2. How do you think a Jewish court might judge this case?

Case Study 2

In 1988, the Israeli newspaper *Yediot Achronot* published a story about a murder that had occurred in 1956. It published the name and pictures of the perpetrator of the crime, who was 61 years old at the time of the article's publication. The former criminal had since been rehabilitated, was married, and ran a successful business. This article exposed his evil past to his neighbors and customers, although there did not appear to be any danger of his acting violently again. He sued the newspaper, claiming that the public exposure of his past life forced him to sell his business and move from the neighborhood, and brought devastating damage to his reputation in the community.

Questions for Discussion:

1. Do you think this suit has any validity?

2. Does the newspaper have the right to disclose personal information in the absence of any compelling public interest?

3. From the perspective of secular law, what rights are pitted against each other in this case?

4. How do you think Jewish law might decide this case?

The Obligation to Preserve the Privacy of Others

Text 1a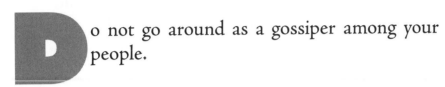

לֹא תֵלֵךְ רָכִיל בְּעַמֶּיךָ

Do not go around as a gossiper among your people.

VAYIKRA/LEVITICUS 19:16

Text 1b

איזהו רכיל?
זה שטוען דברים והולך מזה לזה ואומר:
"כך אמר פלוני, כך וכך שמעתי על פלוני"
אף על פי שהוא אמת וגם אין בו גנות הרי זה עובר בלאו

Who is a gossiper? One who collects information and then goes from person to person, saying, "This is what so and so said; this is what I hear about so and so." Even if the statements are true and are not necessarily disparaging, they constitute a violation of a negative commandment.

RABBI SHLOMO GANZFRIED
KITZUR SHULCHAN ARUCH (ABRIDGED CODE OF JEWISH LAW) 30:1

Rabbi Shlomo Ganzfried (1804–1886), best known for *Kitzur Shulchan Aruch,* summarizing Rabbi Yosef Karo's *Shulchan Aruch* and subsequent commentaries and Jewish Hungarian customs up to the 19th century. It was written "for G-d-fearing Jews not in a position to study and comprehend the (full) *Shulchan Aruch* and commentaries, composed in an easily understood Hebrew" [Title page of the first edition].

Text 2 ▌

מניין לאומר דבר לחבירו שהוא בבל יאמר עד שיאמר לו "לך אמור"?
שנאמר: "וידבר ה' אליו מאהל מועד לאמר"

How do we know that if someone tells something to his friend, the friend may not repeat it unless he was told explicitly that he could say it? Because it says (Vayikra 1:1): And G-d spoke to him [Moses] in the tent, saying [i.e., telling him to repeat it to the people]. . . .

TALMUD, YOMA 4B

Text 3 ▌

מי שבא לפתוח חלון לחצר חבירו
בין חלון גדולה בין חלון קטנה בין למעלה בין למטה
בעל החצר מעכב עליו, שהרי אומר: "תזיק לי בראיה"
ואף על פי שהוא גבוהה תעלה בסולם ותראה

Rabbi Yosef Karo (1488–1575), author of the *Shulchan Aruch* (a definitively authoritative code of Jewish law); *Beit Yosef,* a commentary on *Arba'ah Turim,* on Jewish law; *Kesef Mishneh* on Maimonides' *Mishneh Torah;* and a mystical work, *Magid Mesharim.* Born in Spain, he fled the Inquisition at the age of four with his family.

If someone wants to put a window in a wall facing upon the courtyard of his neighbor, whether it be a large or small window, whether high or low, the owner of the courtyard can prevent him from doing so by claiming that "you will harm me by looking in. Even if it is a high window, you can go up on a ladder and look in on my courtyard."

RABBI YOSEF KARO
SHULCHAN ARUCH (CODE OF JEWISH LAW), CHOSHEN MISHPAT 154:6

Text 4a

מַה טֹּבוּ אֹהָלֶיךָ יַעֲקֹב מִשְׁכְּנֹתֶיךָ יִשְׂרָאֵל

How beautiful are your tents O Jacob; your dwelling places O Israel.

<small>BAMIDBAR/NUMBERS 24:5</small>

Text 4b

"וישא בלעם את עיניו וירא את ישראל שוכן לשבטיו"
מה ראה? ראה שאין פתחי אהליהם מכוונין זה לזה
אמר: ראוין הללו שתשרה עליהם שכינה

Balaam saw how the doorway of the tent of one Jew never faced the doorway of the tent of another Jew. Upon seeing this, Balaam exclaimed: These people deserve that the Divine spirit rest upon them.

<small>TALMUD, BAVA BATRA 60A</small>

Laws Regarding Slander (*Lashon Hara*)
Definition of Slander

Text 5a

Slander is the telling of deprecating facts about a colleague, even if these facts are true. Slander does not refer to someone who invents lies; that is referred to as defamation of character. Rather a slanderer is someone who sits and relates . . . uncomplimentary things. A person who listens to slander is worse than one that shares it.

KITZUR SHULCHAN ARUCH (ABRIDGED CODE OF JEWISH LAW), OP. CIT., 30:2

Text 5b

Slander includes those who make deprecatory remarks in the presence of a colleague or behind his back; those who relate matters which, when passed from one person to another, will cause harm to a colleague's person or his property.

KITZUR SHULCHAN ARUCH (ABRIDGED CODE OF JEWISH LAW), OP. CIT., 30:5

Shades of Slander–*Avak Lashon Hara*

Text 6

זימנין הוה יתיב קמיה וקא פסיק סידרא בספר תהלים
אמר רבי: כמה מיושר כתב זה
אמר ליה: לאו אנא כתבתיה, יהודה חייטא כתביה
אמר ליה: כלך מלשון הרע הזה

Another time, Rabbi Shimon was sitting before Rebbi and Rebbi was finishing a section in the Book of Psalms. Rebbi said, "How neat is this handwriting." Rabbi Shimon replied to him, "I did not write it, Yehudah Chayata wrote it." Rebbi retorted to R. Shimon: "Desist from this slander."

TALMUD, BAVA BATRA 164B

Text 7

There are certain matters which are considered "the shades of slander," for example, someone says: "Do not talk about so and so; I do not want to say what happened." Similarly, it is also considered the "shades of slander" when someone speaks favorably about a colleague in the presence of his enemies, for this will surely prompt them to speak disparagingly about him . . . . Similarly, this category includes a person who relates slander in frivolity and jest, as if he were not speaking with hatred . . . . It also includes someone who slanders a colleague slyly, pretending to be innocently telling a story without knowing that it is slanderous. When he is reproved, he excuses himself by saying: "I did not know that the story was slanderous or that so and so was involved."

KITZUR SHULCHAN ARUCH (ABRIDGED CODE OF JEWISH LAW), OP. CIT., 30:4

Shaming Others

Text 8

It is forbidden to embarrass a colleague, whether by one's statements or by one's deeds . . . in public. Similarly, he should not refer to him by a name which will embarrass him, or relate a story which will embarrass him.

KITZUR SHULCHAN ARUCH (ABRIDGED CODE OF JEWISH LAW), OP. CIT., 29:1

Text 9

כי הא דיתיב רבי וקא דריש והריח ריח שום
אמר: מי שאכל שום-יצא
עמד רבי חייא ויצא. עמדו כולן ויצאו
בשחר מצאו רבי שמעון ברבי לרבי חייא
אמר ליה: אתה הוא שציערת לאבא?
אמר לו: לא תהא כזאת בישראל

Rebbi was sitting and teaching his students and he smelled an odor of garlic. He said, "Whoever ate garlic should leave." So Rabbi

Chiya rose and left. Immediately, all the other students rose and left.

The following morning, Rabbi Shimon the son of Rebbi met Rabbi Chiya and said, "Was it you who irritated my father with your bad breath?" Rabbi Chiya replied, "Heaven forbid. I would never eat garlic before coming to the study hall. I left in order to save the guilty party from embarrassment."

TALMUD, SANHEDRIN 11A

What's So Bad About Negative Talk?
Dangerous Talk

Text 10a

מָוֶת וְחַיִּים בְּיַד לָשׁוֹן

Death and life are in the hands of the tongue.

MISHLEI/PROVERBS 18:21

Text 10b

דאמר רבא: דבעי חיים בלישניה, דבעי מיתה בלישניה

Rava said: the one who wants life should turn to his tongue. The one who wants death should turn to his tongue.

TALMUD, ARACHIN 15B

Text 10c 📜

אמר רבי חמא ברבי חנינא:

מאי דכתיב: "מות וחיים ביד לשון"? וכי יש יד ללשון?

לומר לך מה יד ממיתה, אף לשון ממיתה

אי מה יד אינה ממיתה אלא בסמוך להאף לשון אינה ממיתה אלא בסמוך לה?

תלמוד לומר: "חץ שחוט לשונם"

אי מה חץ עד ארבעים וחמשים אמה, אף לשון עד ארבעים וחמשים אמה?

תלמוד לומר: "שתו בשמים פיהם ולשונם תהלך בארץ"

Rabbi Chama the son of Rabbi Chanina says: What does the verse mean when it says life and death are in the hand of the tongue? Does the tongue have hands? This is to teach us that just as a hand can kill, so can a tongue.

Is a tongue limited to kill in close proximity, like a hand? The verse says "Their tongue is a sharpened arrow (Yirmiyahu/Jeremiah 9:7)."

Is the tongue limited to a distance of forty or fifty cubits, like an arrow? The verse says, "They placed their mouth in the skies [i.e., the limit of the damage of the tongue is the sky]."

TALMUD, ARACHIN 15B

Text 10d

לשון תליתאי קטיל תליתאי: הורג למספרו ולמקבלו ולאומרו

Slander kills three: the speaker, the listener and the one being slandered.

TALMUD, ARACHIN 15B

Speech Reflects Inner Character

Text 11

הנהו תלתא כהני
חד אמר להו: הגיעני כפול
וחד אמר: הגיעני כזית
וחד אמר: הגיעני כזנב הלטאה
בדקו אחריו ומצאו בו שמץ פסול

There were three *kohanim* [who had each received a share of the show bread]. One said to the others, "[A piece] the size of a bean reached me." One said, "[A piece] the size of an olive reached me." And one said "[A piece] the size of a lizard's tail reached me." They investigated the third one, and found in him some disqualifying flaw.

TALMUD, PESACHIM 3B

Speech Shapes Inner Character

Text 12a

וַיִּיצֶר ה׳ אֱלֹקִים אֶת הָאָדָם עָפָר מִן הָאֲדָמָה
וַיִּפַּח בְּאַפָּיו נִשְׁמַת חַיִּים וַיְהִי הָאָדָם לְנֶפֶשׁ חַיָּה

And G-d formed man from dust from the ground, and he blew into his nostrils the breath of life, and man became a living soul.

BEREISHIT/GENESIS 2:7

Text 12b

והות באדם לרוח ממללא

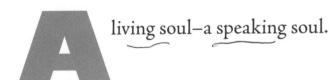

A living soul—a speaking soul.

ONKELOS

Onkelos (circa 35-120 CE) was a famous convert to Judaism and a student of the sages of the *Mishnah*. According to traditional Jewish sources, he was a prominent Roman nobleman, a nephew of the Roman emperor. He was the author of the *Targum Onkelos*, an Aramaic translation of the Torah (c. 110 CE).

Text 13a

Every intellectual idea that emerges from the source of intellect appears in a measured and limited form . . . in breadth and depth. But when it takes the form of speech, we see clearly that the idea expands immensely, far surpassing its prior state when it emerged from the intellect into the language of thought. For [when in the domain of thought] it is still constricted and confined within certain parameters but when it is verbalized, it expands immensely with many details and ramifications, incomparably surpassing its initial stage in the words of thought.

RABBI SHALOM DOVBER SCHNEERSOHN, SEFER HAMA'AMARIM 5658 [1898]

Text 13b

This ability of speech appears in the realms of emotion as well. For instance, when one speaks words of love—which means that the speech is being informed by the soul's attribute of love—we see that speaking intensifies the love. This is because speaking of the love causes it to illuminate intensely within the person, who then grows very passionate with love and affection for the object of his love.

The same is true of severity and anger: Speech fuels the passion of anger and rage immensely. Thus [the author of] *Reishit Chochmah* advises silence as an antidote to anger since speech increases the passion of the anger immensely. Silence, on the other hand, has the opposite effect; it cools the passion of rage.

The same is true of all the emotions. If they are not verbalized, their excitement will gradually dissipate until they vanish entirely. When they are verbalized, the opposite occurs: they grow and expand immensely.

IBID.

Text 13c

This is why one must study Torah aloud, as the verse says, "and you shall speak of them (Devarim/Deuteronomy 6:7)." It is also written, "[The words of Torah] are life to he that finds them (Proverbs 4:22)," [as our sages explain], "to he that articulates them with the mouth." For when one studies a given *halachah* [Torah law] aloud, he will develop new insights into the depth of the *halachah,* insights that would not have occurred to him had he merely pondered the *halachah* in his mind without actually saying it . . . .

Likewise in the service of prayer, in which expressing the letters and words of the prayers *verbally* is primary. Now the utterance of the prayers must be accompanied by meditation; then, with the actual uttering of the words, the light of the prayers is felt in one's soul more than through meditation alone.

Ibid.

Text 14

אמר רב חנן בר רב: הכל יודעין כלה למה נכנסה לחופה
אלא כל המנבל פיו ומוציא דבר נבלה מפיו
אפילו נחתם לו גזר דינו של שבעים שנה לטובה, נהפך עליו לרעה

Rav Chanan Bar Rav says: All know why a bride enters the bridal chamber, but if anyone talks obscenely and brings forth an obscene word from his mouth, even if a decree of seventy years of good was sealed for him, it is turned for him into evil.

TALMUD, KETUBOT 8B

Speech Creates Reality (Mystical View)

Text 15

A resident of Mezibuzh had a quarrel with another. Once, while in the Baal Shem Tov's *shul*, he shouted that he would tear the other person to pieces like a fish.

The Baal Shem Tov told his pupils to hold one another's hands, and to stand near him with their eyes closed. Then he placed his holy hands on the shoulders of the two disciples next to him. Suddenly the disciples began shouting in great terror: They had seen that fellow actually dismembering his disputant. This incident shows clearly that every potential has an effect—either in physical form or on a spiritual plane that can be perceived only with higher and more refined senses.

RABBI MENACHEM MENDEL SCHNEERSON (THE LUBAVITCHER REBBE)
HAYOM YOM, TISHREI 29

Rabbi Menachem Mendel Schneerson (1902–1994), "the Lubavitcher Rebbe," also known simply as "the Rebbe." Born in southern Ukraine. Rabbi Schneerson escaped from the Nazis, arriving in the US in June 1941. The Rebbe, the towering Jewish leader of the twentieth century, inspired and guided the revival of traditional Judaism after the European devastation, and often emphasized that the performance of just one additional good deed could usher in the era of Mashiach.

Text 16 🕮

אין העולם מתקיים אלא בשביל הבל תינוקות של בית רבן
אמר ליה רב פפא לאביי: דידי ודידך מאי?
אמר ליה: אינו דומה הבל שיש בו חטא, להבל שאין בו חטא

The world exists because of the breath of school-children [who utter words of Torah]. Rav Pappa said to Abaye: And my and your words of Torah are not sufficient? Abaye said: We cannot compare the breath of a mouth that was tainted by sin to the breath of a mouth that is not tainted by sin.

TALMUD, SHABBAT 119B

Text 17 🕮

The world is in need of a purified atmosphere. Purified air comes only through words of Torah . . . . Purification of the air is the task of every person familiar with Torah and Torah literature, and is effected through the letters of Torah. When reciting words of Torah while in the store or walking in the street or riding the subway, one cleans the air [in a spiritual sense].

HAYOM YOM, TEVET 11/SIVAN 9, OP. CIT.

Case Studies: Competing Values

Case Study 3

Dear Rabbi Kushelevitz,

I am an accountant of a big corporation, and in the process of doing the company's books, I realized that a secretary was embezzling funds. I had warned the secretary on several occasions, to no avail. I have the option to make his behavior public by announcing my findings at the next board meeting in front of all the corporate officers. Of course, the secretary would be present as well. I see this as the only alternative to stop the secretary from future embezzlements. Do I have an obligation to let the company know that one of their employees is a thief?

RABBI SHMUEL KUSHELEVITZ, SHA'ALOT UTESHUVOT NETIV SHMUEL, NO. 9

Case Study 4

Dear Rabbi Waldenberg,

I am an optometrist who became aware that one of my patients recently developed a visual impairment. He asked me not to tell anyone and assured me that he will not drive a car anymore. However, I have a suspicion that he is not truthful and does plan to drive. Do I have an obligation to tell the Department of Motor Vehicles that the patient is not safe on the road and should be denied a license to drive?

RABBI ELIEZER WALDENBERG, TZITZ ELIEZER, VOL.15, NO. 13

Case Study 5

Dear Rabbi Breish,

I am a physician of a boy who is engaged to be married. Over the course of a routine checkup I discovered that he had a tumor that was likely to kill him within a year or two. My colleagues and I did not tell the patient about it, as we fear that the shock may worsen his condition. Am I ethically obligated to tell the family of the bride, or am I bound to preserve the confidence of the patient?

RABBI MORDECHAI YA'AKOV BREISH, CHELKAT YA'AKOV, VOL. 3, NO. 136

Rabbi Eliezer Yehudah Waldenberg (1915–2006), of Jerusalem, leading rabbi and a *Dayan* on the Supreme Rabbinical Court in Jerusalem, considered an eminent authority on medical halachah. He was the author of a monumental halachic treatise, *Tzitz Eliezer,* that covers a wide breadth of Jewish law including Jewish medical ethics, an encyclopedic treatise on halachic questions; it is viewed as one of the great achievements of halachic scholarship of the 20th century. He was the rabbi of the Shaare Zedek Medical Center in Jerusalem.

Rabbi Mordechai Ya'akov Breish (1895–1976), Chief Rabbi and Head of the Rabbinical Court of Zurich from 1934-1976, Author of *Chelkat Yaakov,* a compendium of responsa on contemporary issues and medical ethics.

Text 18

כל היכול להציל ולא הציל עובר על "לא תעמוד על דם רעך"

וכן הרואה את חבירו טובע בים

או ליסטים באים עליו או חיה רעה באה עליו

ויכול להצילו הוא בעצמו או שישכור אחרים להצילו ולא הציל

או ששמע גוים או מוסרים מחשבים עליו רעה או טומנין לו פח

ולא גלה אוזן חבירו והודיעו

או שידע בגוי או באנס שהוא קובל על חבירו

ויכול לפייסו בגלל חבירו ולהסיר מה שבלבו ולא פייסו

וכל כיוצא בדברים אלו, העושה אותם עובר על "לא תעמוד על דם רעך"

Anyone who can save his friend [from danger] and does not save him is in violation of the verse, "Do not stand idly by the blood of your fellow." Therefore, if someone sees a friend drowning in a sea, or being attacked by robbers, and he is able to save him; or he heard that people were plotting to cause him harm, or planning to entrap him, and he does not reveal it to his friend, he is in violation of that verse

• • • •

RAMBAM, MISHNEH TORAH, HILCHOT ROTZE'ACH (LAWS OF MURDER) 1:14

Rabbi Moshe ben Maimon (1135–1204), better known as Maimonides or Rambam, author of *Mishneh Torah*, a compendium of Jewish law, and *Guide for the Perplexed*. He was born in Córdoba, Spain. After the conquest of Córdoba by the Almohads, who sought to forcibly convert the Jews to Islam, he fled and eventually settled in Cairo. There he became the leader of the Jewish community and served as court physician to the vizier of Egypt.

Text 19

כי הא דטוביה חטא ואתא זיגוד לחודיה ואסהיד ביה קמיה דרב פפא
נגדיה לזיגוד. אמר ליה: "טוביה חטא וזיגוד מינגד?"
אמר ליה: "אין. דכתיב: "לא יקום עד אחד באיש", ואת לחודך אסהדת ביה
שם רע בעלמא קא מפקת ביה"

A ny negative report which does not provide any constructive purpose of justice is
deemed immoral.

Tuviah transgressed and Zigud came by himself and
testified against him before the Rabbinical Court of
Rav Pappa. Rav Pappa, instead of punishing Tuviah,
punished Zigud.

Zigud said to Rav Pappa, "Tuviah sinned and Zigud
was punished?"

Rav Pappa replied, "Yes indeed, for it is written: 'A single
witness shall not stand up to testify against any man [i.e.,
we do not rely on the testimony of a lone witness](Devarim
19:15),' and you have testified against him by yourself.
Thus, your testimony is unacceptable in court. By making your statement, you have put forth a simple slander
against him which is deserving of punishment in court."

TALMUD, PESACHIM 113A

Learning to Use Words Well
Two Approaches to Transforming Speech

Text 20

We have a tradition attributed to the Baal Shem Tov: When one hears an uncomplimentary report about another Jew, even if he does not know the individual referred to, he should be deeply pained. For one of the two is certainly in the wrong: If what they are saying about the individual is true, then he is defective; and if it is not true, then the talebearer is in an unhealthy situation.

HAYOM YOM, KISLEV 12, OP. CIT.

Key Points

1. Speech is the faculty that most distinguishes humans from animals. Rooted in the essence of our being, it affects our thoughts and emotions. The effects of speech are far-reaching—capable of affecting even life and death at distances far greater than is the possible potential of any physical action.

2. Crude, obscene, or pessimistic language does not always directly hurt others, but its negativity disrupts our own personal integrity.

3. Speech has the effects of revealing potential and actualizing. Its effect on the environment is even physical: created by the formation of air, the spiritual content of our speech directly impacts the atmosphere around us.

4. The way in which we speak to—and about—others has a profound effect on how their personalities are revealed, whether for good or ill.

5. Gossip, or *rechilut*, is the peddling of information about others and is forbidden by Torah law. It is considered a violation of privacy. It can cause damage even when true and even when it implies no criticism.

6. Slander, or *lashon hara*, means relating negative information, and it is forbidden. Insinuation or excessive praise are each forbidden as well because they can lead to *lashon hara* or negative repercussions against the person being spoken about.

7. We are required to divulge constructive information if there is no other way to correct wrongdoing or to save innocent victims from danger.

8. The *Mussar* school focuses on behavioral response to limit the negative effects of gossip and slander, while the approach of *Chasidut* is to attack gossip and slander at its root. *Chasidut* emphasizes that when loving feelings are nurtured, gossip and slander naturally fade away.

Additional Readings

Free Speech

By **Rabbi Berel Wein**

Free speech is an integral part of a free society. Yet, like all freedoms, it requires responsibility and self-discipline in its exercise. Justice Oliver Wendell Holmes, in his famous Supreme Court opinion, declared that freedom of speech does not allow one to shout "fire" in a crowded theater where no fire exists. Thus, even this most free of all our freedoms, the right to say what we wish, must be subject to some limitations in order for society to function.

Nevertheless, we are witness daily to outrageous slanders, both personal and communal, that fill our media. Gossip columnists are folk heroes even if they are consistently wrong and vicious in their reports. We are so enamored of the affairs of others that the concept of the right to personal privacy, especially for people in the public eye, has been shredded. Personal attacks, slanderous statements, and dubious opinions about others are all now acceptable in our society. The cost of such behavior is, in my opinion, inestimable, and it is the source of much of what is wrong in Jewish life in America and Israel today.

The Torah deals with wretched types of dermatological diseases (whatever they were, they did not include leprosy) that require spiritual cleansing in order for the afflicted person to be healed and to become ritually pure once more. Our Rabbis stated that these diseases were caused by a spiritual failing—the sin of lashon hara, "evil speech." The Torah bids us not to speak about other human beings. The Talmud indicates that there are instances when even apparently complimentary speech about others is not permitted. We all know how derogatory faint praise and snide compliments can be. The Talmud realized that this problem of uninhibited freedom of speech was so all-encompassing that it stated that all human beings are somehow covered by the "dust of lashon hara." In the last century, the sainted Rabbi Yisrael Meir Kagan wrote a number of great books detailing the laws of speech and how to avoid the trap of speaking lashon hara. A great effort was made, and is still being made, in the traditional Jewish world to speak in an acceptable and refined holy fashion. There is no room

for slander in life. The *exposé,* whether oral or in print, usually leaves the speaker more exposed than the victim. Our rabbis taught us that lashon hara "kills" three victims —the speaker, the listener, and the subject of the conversation. Uninhibited speech leads to bad consequences.

The characteristic that distinguishes humans from animals is the power of speech, which, more than any other trait, represents our intellectual capacity to communicate. Judaism always has taught that this characteristic is a holy gift from the Creator. Just like the gifts of life, health, talents, and family, this gift of speech is not to be abused. It is to be used sparingly and carefully, for good purposes and not for evil. Gossip, muckraking, slander, and cynical language all fly in the face of the purpose of this holy gift of speech. Even when one is speaking the truth, one is cautioned to avoid the pitfalls of lashon hara, for unlike the case of a libel action, truth alone is not a sufficient cause for speaking about others. As such, the rabbinic encouragement of healthy silence is well understood and appreciated. In a world where, sadly, this precept is in vogue, and in fact, the entire concept of lashon hara may inspire only incredulity, a determined effort on our part to restore the sanctity of speech is certainly in order.

Lesson 5
The Truth, The Whole Truth, and Nothing But The Truth
Balancing the Values of Honesty and Fairness

Introduction

The divine seal, the sages tell us, is *emet*, or truth. Yet in a world in which good and evil must coexist, an unwavering devotion to truth may seem naïve, even counterproductive.

How are we to discern its correct application and decide when honesty really *is* the best policy?

אמת
(Truth)

Is Honesty the Best Policy?

Learning Activity 1

Decide in each case whether lying is always justified, usually justified, sometimes justified, or never justified.

Based on your responses, be prepared to discuss the questions following the activity.

Is it right to lie in order to	Always	Usually	Sometimes	Never
get hired by a firm suspected of polluting, in order to gather evidence?				
keep one's landlord from knowing you have a cat?				
keep secret a crime you committed ten years ago that you deeply regret?				
get a job at a law firm by claiming to have graduated from an Ivy League school?				
get out of helping a friend to move?				
keep from hurting your parents' feelings?				
avoid an embarrassing admission of ignorance?				
keep a friend from discovering preparations for a surprise party?				
keep a sick man from knowing he is dying?				
protect young children from a frightening truth?				

Questions for Discussion

1. Which lies are always justified?

2. Which are never justified?

3. Can you formulate a general rule about when lying might be the more ethical choice and when it is definitely wrong?

American vs. Jewish Legal Systems

Text 1 📖

מנין לדיין שיודע בדין שהוא מרומה
שלא יאמר: "הואיל והעדים מעידין
אחתכנו ויהא קולר תלוי בצואר עדים"?
תלמוד לומר: "מדבר שקר תרחק"

f a judge feels that a witness is deceptive, he should not say, "I will decide the case based on the strict principles of the Law, and let the blame [for possible injustice] fall upon the witnesses," for it says, "You shall distance yourself from falsehood (Shemot/Exodus 23:7)."

TALMUD, SHEVU'OT 31A

Case Study

Dear Rabbi Yosef,

I am a member of a group of three judges who are involved in arbitrating a monetary dispute between two members of our community. My view differed with my other colleagues in the *bet din*. Thus, the majority of opinions seemed to be leaning towards a position which I felt was utterly mistaken. I feel that by bringing in more judges the case will gain from the input of the additional judges, hopefully leading to a just verdict. Is it right for me to be deceptive and say that I don't have an answer in order to force the other members to invite two more judges?

RABBI OVADIAH YOSEF, YABIA OMER, VOL. 2, CHOSHEN MISHPAT, NO. 3

Rabbi Ovadiah Yosef (1920–), born in Basra, Iraq. Talmudic scholar, a recognized authority in Halachah, former Sephardic Chief Rabbi of Israel. He is revered for his erudition and Torah scholarship.

Defining Honesty
Who's Lying?

Learning Activity 2

With a partner, consider each of the scenarios and decide whether a lie is being told.

1. If someone is delusional and tells outlandish stories, would we consider that person a liar?

2. If I tell a joke and everyone knows that I am joking, is this a lie?

3. I visit a new town and tell people my name is Harry. Really my name is Joe. No one is harmed by this lie; they do not know me. I am not concealing a past nor impersonating anyone. Is this a lie?

4. A teacher accuses a student of not having studied for a test. The student, in a hurt and sarcastic voice, answers, "Of course I haven't studied. I haven't spent even a minute looking at the material," thus implying by her tone that she has been misjudged. In fact, the student has not studied. Is the student lying?

Deception as the Core of Lying

Text 2 ▌

הקדוש ברוך הוא שונאן: המדבר אחד בפה ואחד בלב . . .

G-d abhors . . . those who speak one thing while another thing is in their hearts.

TALMUD, PESACHIM 113B

Text 3 ▌

אסור לאדם להנהיג עצמו בדברי חלקות ופיתוי
ולא יהיה אחד בפה ואחד בלב . . .
ולא יסרהב בחבירו שיאכל אצלו והוא יודע שאינו אוכל

It is forbidden to accustom oneself to smooth speech and flatteries. One must not say one thing and mean another . . . one must not urge another to join him at a meal, when he is aware that the invitation will not be accepted. Nor should one press upon another any marks of friendship which one knows will be declined.

RAMBAM, MISHNEH TORAH, HILCHOT DE'OT (LAWS OF DISPOSITIONS) 2:6

R. Moshe ben Maimon (1135–1204), better known as Maimonides or Rambam, author of *Mishneh Torah*, a compendium of Jewish law, and *Guide for the Perplexed*. He was born in Córdoba, Spain. After the conquest of Córdoba by the Almohads, who sought to forcibly convert the Jews to Islam, he fled and eventually settled in Cairo. There he became the leader of the Jewish community and served as court physician to the vizier of Egypt.

Why Tell the Truth?
Pragmatic Benefits

Text 4

Suppose men imagined there was no obligation to veracity, and acted accordingly; speaking as often against their own opinion as according to it; would not all pleasure of conversation be destroyed, and all confidence in narration? Men would only speak in bargaining and in this too would soon lose all mutual confidence.

FRANCIS HUTCHESON, A SYSTEM OF MORAL PHILOSOPHY

Francis Hutcheson (1694–1746), philosopher, one of the founding fathers of the Scottish Enlightenment. His importance is due almost entirely to his ethical writings.

Text 5

מה טיבו של בדאי הזה
אפילו אומר דברים של אמת אין מאמינים אותו

Thus is the life of the deceiver: even when he speaks the truth he is not believed.

MIDRASH, BEREISHIT RABAH, 94:3

Text 6 🗎

Rabbi Yitzchak Abuhav (14th century), was a Talmudic scholar, who toward the end of his life devoted much time to literary work and preaching. He wrote *Menorat HaMaor* ("The Candlestick of Light") for his own use as a public speaker. It has probably contributed more than any other medieval book to popularizing Torah knowledge, with Agadic material from the religious and ethical points of view.

Lying can cause quarrel, strife, murder, vain oaths, and many other transgressions

. . . . All these evils stem from speaking falsehood. Therefore the Torah says: "Distance yourself from lies," (Exodus 23:7) and immediately it states: "Do not kill the innocent with the righteous." (Exodus 23:7) This instructs us that lies lead to killing the innocent. Therefore, happy is the person who distances himself from them, and trains his mouth to speak truth, humility, and right. Through this he will attain his desire: a good path in this world and in the world to come; he will guide his household in the straight path and will be saved from all trouble.

RABBI YITZCHAK ABUHAV, MENORAT HAMAOR

Honesty as a G-dly Virtue

Text 7 🗎

חותמו של הקדוש ברוך הוא אמת

The seal of the Blessed Holy One is truth.

TALMUD, YOMA 69B; SANHEDRIN 64A; SHABBAT 58A

Text 8

שורש המצוה ידוע, כי השקר נתעב ונאלח בעיני הכל
אין דבר מאוס ממנו, והמארה והקללות בבית כל אוהביו
מפני שהשם יתברך א–ל אמת וכל אשר אתו אמת
ואין הברכה מצויה וחלה אלא במתדמים אליו במעשיהם
להיותם אמיתיים כמו שהוא א–ל אמת
ולהיותם מרחמים כמו שידוע שהוא רחום
ולהיותם גומלי חסדים כמו שהוא רב החסד

The root of this Mitzvah is that falsehood is repulsed by all; there is nothing more objectionable then lying. Those who love the quality of falsehood are not eligible for His blessings, for He is true and everything about Him is true. His blessings can only be bestowed upon those who emulate Him in their actions that they be truthful, just as He is true; and to be compassionate as He is, etc.

RABBI AHARON HALEVI, SEFER HACHINUCH, NO. 74

Rabbi Aharon HaLevi of Barceiona (1235–1290) was a Talmudic scholar and *Halachist.* Some are of the opinion that he is the author of the anonymous *Sefer HaChinuch,* although some historians do not agree with this attribution.

Text 9

הוא שהנביא אומר וה' אלהים אמת
הוא לבדו האמת ואין לאחר אמת כאמתתו
והוא שהתורה אומרת אין עוד מלבדו
כלומר אין שם מצוי אמת מלבדו כמותו

One of the Prophets said, "But the L-rd is the true G-d," meaning that only G-d is everlasting and that nothing else is. This is what the

Torah has said: "There is none else beside Him," namely, that there is nothing in existence that is everlasting, except for G-d.

Mishneh Torah, op. cit., Hilchot Yesodei Hatorah (Foundations of Torah), 1:4

Truth as the Underlying Force of All Existence

Text 10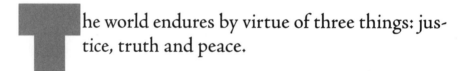

עַל שְׁלשָׁה דְבָרִים הָעוֹלָם עוֹמֵד עַל הַדִּין וְעַל הָאֱמֶת וְעַל הַשָּׁלוֹם

The world endures by virtue of three things: justice, truth and peace.

Mishnah, Avot 1:18

Truth in the Real World
Truths That Cause Damage

Text 11

It is only the cynic who claims to "speak the truth" at all times and in all places to all men in the same way but who, in fact, develops nothing but a lifeless image of the truth. He dons the halo of the fanatical devotee of truth who can make no allowances for human weaknesses; but, in fact, he is destroying the living truth between men. He wounds shame, desecrates mystery, breaks confidence, betrays the community in which he lives.

DIETRICH BONHOEFFER, WHAT IS MEANT BY "TELLING THE TRUTH"

Dietrich Bonhoeffer (1906–1945) was a German Lutheran theologian and participant in the German Resistance movement against Nazism. He was involved in plots planned by members of the Abwehr (the German Military Intelligence Office) to assassinate Hitler. He was arrested in 1943, imprisoned, and eventually hanged just before the end of World War II.

Lying for the Sake of Peace

Text 12

בשעה שבא הקדוש ברוך הוא לבראת את אדם הראשון
נעשו מלאכי השרת כיתים כיתים, וחבורות חבורות
מהם אומרים אל יברא ומהם אומרים יברא . . .
חסד אומר יברא שהוא גומל חסדים
ואמת אומר אל יברא שכולו שקרים
צדק אומר יברא שהוא עושה צדקות
שלום אומר אל יברא דכוליה קטטה
מה עשה הקדוש ברוך הוא? נטל אמת והשליכו לארץ

Rabbi Simon says, "When G-d was about to create Adam, the angels on high divided into different camps. Some said he should not be created; others said he should be created.

Kindness said, 'Let him be created, for he will be generous and kind.'

Truth said, 'Do not create him for he will be full of lies.'

Righteousness said, 'Create him for he will do charity and righteousness.'

Peace said, 'Do not create him for he is full of conflict.'

So G-d took Truth and threw it to the ground, and then created man."

BEREISHIT RABAH, OP. CIT., 8:5

Praising a Bride

Text 13

כֵּיצַד מְרַקְּדִין לִפְנֵי הַכַּלָּה?

בֵּית שַׁמַּאי אוֹמְרִים: אוֹמְרִים כַּלָּה כְּמוֹת שֶׁהִיא

וּבֵית הִלֵּל אוֹמְרִים: כַּלָּה נָאָה וַחֲסוּדָה

אָמְרוּ לָהֶן בֵּית שַׁמַּאי לְבֵית הִלֵּל: הֲרֵי שֶׁהָיְתָה חִיגֶּרֶת אוֹ סוּמָא

וְהַתּוֹרָה אָמְרָה: "מִדְּבַר שֶׁקֶר תִּרְחָק", אוֹמְרִים לָהּ: כַּלָּה נָאָה וַחֲסוּדָה?

אָמְרוּ לָהֶם בֵּית הִלֵּל לְבֵית שַׁמַּאי: לְדִבְרֵיכֶם: מִי שֶׁלָּקַח מֶקַח רַע מִן הַשּׁוּק

יְשַׁבְּחֶנּוּ בְּעֵינָיו אוֹ יְגַנֶּנּוּ בְּעֵינָיו? הֱוֵי אוֹמֵר: יְשַׁבְּחֶנּוּ בְּעֵינָיו

מִכָּאן אָמְרוּ חֲכָמִים: לְעוֹלָם תְּהֵא דַּעְתּוֹ שֶׁל אָדָם מְעוֹרֶבֶת עִם הַבְּרִיּוֹת

ur rabbis taught, "How do we dance before the bride? What songs do the dancers sing while they dance? The academy of Shammai says, 'They sing the praises of each bride as she is [i.e., the dancers only sing about the positive qualities with which the bride is endowed, avoiding anything untrue or exaggerated].'

But the academy of Hillel says, 'We treat every bride as if she is beautiful and sing before her, "A beautiful and graceful bride."' The sages of Shammai's academy said to those of Hillel's, 'If she was lame or blind, do we say about her, 'a beautiful and graceful bride?'" But the Torah states, 'Keep far from a false matter!'

The sages of Hillel's academy said to those of Shammai's, 'According to your words, if someone has made a bad purchase in the marketplace, should one praise it in his eyes or criticize it in his eyes? You must say, "He should praise it in his eyes."' From here the Sages said, 'A person's disposition toward people should always be congenial.'"

TALMUD, KETUVOT 16B-17A

Withholding the Truth from a Dying Person

Text 14a

מי שחלה ונטה למות אומרים לו: התודה

A person who is dying is told to confess.

TALMUD, SHABBAT 32A

Text 14b

אומרים לו: התודה
ואומרים לו: הרבה התודו ולא מתו והרבה שלא התודו מתו
ובשכר שאתה מתודה אתה חי

In order to prevent breaking his heart [causing deterioration of the person's condition and expediting the process of death], we tell him/her, "Many confessed on their death bed and didn't die in the end . . . in the merit of your repentance you will live."

RABBI YOSEF KARO, SHULCHAN ARUCH (CODE OF JEWISH LAW), YOREH DE'AH 338:1

Rabbi Yosef Karo (1488–1575), author of the *Shulchan Aruch* (a definitively authoritative code of Jewish law); *Beit Yosef,* a commentary on *Arba'ah Turim,* on Jewish law; *Kesef Mishneh* on Maimonides' *Mishneh Torah;* and a mystical work, *Magid Mesharim.* Born in Spain, he fled the Inquisition at the age of four with his family.

Text 14c

It is clear that one may not disclose the true condition of the illness to the critically ill, in order not to cause shock and to give hope so he would continue to pray ("Even if a sword is resting on his neck, one should not give up hope and prayer," Talmud, Berachot 10a). Hence, if the doctors determined that the person has cancer, one should refrain from disclosing the full diagnosis to the patient. Even if a parent demands of their child to disclose all the information, it is forbidden to do so, if there is a chance that it will generate despair or unnecessary anguish to the parent.

RABBI BETZALEL STERN, BETZEL HACHOCHMAH, VOL. 2, NO. 55

Text 14d

Not only withholding information is permitted, but also stating that the patient will get better—even if it is highly uncertain—may be necessary if the condition of the sick person requires it. One is permitted to lie to save a life.

RABBI Y.L. GINZBURG, MOSAD HANEVI'IM

Rabbi Yehudah HeChasid of Regensburg (1150-1217), was a Talmudic scholar, mystic, and Kabbalist. He was the leader of *Chasidei Ashkenaz*, a pietistic group of scholars and mystics. He wrote *Sefer Chasidim* (*"Book of the Pious"*), a guidebook of the religious life of medieval German Jews. Many of his teachings and customs have been incorporated into standard Halachic Jewish practice.

Text 14e

If someone is in great pain and wishes to die, it is permitted to tell him the truth, as this is a comfort to the patient. Likewise if he is very old and/or says that he is not afraid of dying, but wishes to know the truth so that he may leave some guidance or counsel to his children, one is permitted to tell the truth.

RABBI YEHUDAH HECHASID, SEFER CHASIDIM, 154

Lying Should Go Against the Grain of Our Personalities

Text 15

רב הוה קא מצערא ליה דביתהו

כי אמר לה עבידי לי טלופחי–עבדא ליה חימצי

חימצי–עבדא ליה טלופחי

כי גדל חייא בריה, אפיך לה

אמר ליה: "איעליא לך אמך"

אמר ליה: אנא הוא דקא אפיכנא לה

אמר ליה: "היינו דקא אמרי אינשי: "דנפיק מינך טעמא מלפך"

את לא תעביד הכי, שנאמר: "למדו לשונם דבר שקר העוה וגו'"

Rav's wife would [deliberately] aggravate him. When he would tell her, "Prepare me lentils," she would instead prepare peas. If he said, "Prepare me peas," she would instead prepare lentils. When his son Chiya grew up and would relay his father's requests to his mother, he would reverse them to her so that his father would end up receiving exactly what he requested. Upon receiving the desired dish, and not realizing Chiya's subterfuge, Rav said to him: "Your mother has improved her ways!" So Chiya replied to him, "It was actually I who reversed your requests to her."

Rav replied to him: "This bears out the popular saying—the child who comes from you will educate you. I too should have thought of this trick. However, you should not do this for it says: 'They train their tongue to speak falsehoods, striving to be iniquitous (Yirmiyahu/Jeremiah 9:4).'"

Talmud, Yevamot 63a

The Extreme Standard of Truth in the Context of Justice
Distancing Oneself from Falsehood

Text 16a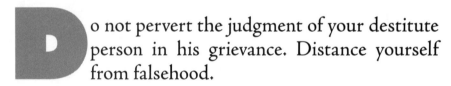

לֹא תַטֶּה מִשְׁפַּט אֶבְיֹנְךָ בְּרִיבוֹ
מִדְּבַר שֶׁקֶר תִּרְחָק

Do not pervert the judgment of your destitute person in his grievance. Distance yourself from falsehood.

SHEMOT/EXODUS 23:7

Text 16b

מנין לתלמיד שאמר לו רבו:
יודע אתה בי שאם נותנין לי מאה מנה איני מבדה
מנה יש לי אצל פלוני ואין לי עליו אלא עד אחד
מנין שלא יצטרף עמו?
תלמוד לומר: "מדבר שקר תרחק"

האי מדבר שקר תרחק נפקא?
הא ודאי שקורי קא משקר, ורחמנא אמר: "לא תענה ברעך עד שקר"
אלא כגון דאמר ליה: ודאי חד סהדא אית לי
ותא אתה קום התם ולא תימא ולא מידי
דהא לא מפקת מפומך שקרא אפילו הכי אסור
משום שנאמר: "מדבר שקר תרחק"

מנין לשנים שבאו לדין אחד לבוש סמרטוטין
ואחד לבוש איצטלית בת מאה מנה
שאומרין לו: לבוש כמותו או הלבישהו כמותך?
תלמוד לומר: "מדבר שקר תרחק"

כי הוו אתו לקמיה דרבא בר רב הונא
אמר להו: שלופו פוזמוקייכו וחותו לדינא

מנין לדיין שלא ישמע דברי בעל דין קודם שיבא בעל דין חבירו?
תלמוד לומר: "מדבר שקר תרחק"

From where is it derived that if a teacher tells his student, "You know about me that even if I would be given a hundred *manehs*, I would not tell a lie. Now, I am owed a *maneh* by so-and-so, but I have only one witness to testify against him," that the student should not join the witness? The Torah states, "Distance yourself from falsehood."

Is this law derived from the verse, "Distance yourself from falsehood?" In such a case, the student would certainly be lying, since he did not witness the alleged loan. And the Merciful One states in His Torah: You shall not testify falsely against your fellow.

Rather, this refers to a case where the teacher said to the student, "I certainly have one witness. Come to court and stand there together with him. But do not say anything, for then you will not utter a falsehood. [By standing with the witness, you will help give the impression that I have two witnesses to support my case. The debtor might therefore be prompted to admit the truth. (Rashi)]". Even in such a case it is prohibited for the student to obey because it is stated: "Distance yourself from falsehood."

From where is it derived that if two litigants come for judgment, one dressed in rags and one wearing an exquisite garment worth one hundred *manehs*, we tell [the well-dressed one] "Dress like him or dress him like you [so that the court will not be disposed toward the well-dressed one. (Rashi)]"? The Torah states, "Distance yourself from falsehood."

When litigants came before Raba bar Rav Huna, he would say to them, "Remove your fine footwear and then go down to judgment!"

From where is it derived that one litigant should not clarify his case to the judge before his opponent arrives? [A litigant who argues his case without his opponent being present will not feel ashamed about lying.] The Torah states, "Distance yourself from falsehood."

TALMUD, SHEVU'OT 31A

A Judge's Dishonesty for the Sake of Justice

Text 17

לֹא תַעֲשׂוּ עָוֶל בַּמִּשְׁפָּט

Do not cause perversion of the justice.

VAYIKRA/LEVITICUS 19:15

Reprise: A Future of Perfect Truth

Text 18 📜

בשעה שבא הקדוש ברוך הוא לבראת את אדם הראשון
נעשו מלאכי השרת כיתים כיתים, וחבורות חבורות
מהם אומרים אל יברא ומהם אומרים יברא . . .
חסד אומר יברא שהוא גומל חסדים
ואמת אומר אל יברא שכולו שקרים
צדק אומר יברא שהוא עושה צדקות
שלום אומר אל יברא דכוליה קטטה
מה עשה הקדוש ברוך הוא? נטל אמת והשליכו לארץ
אמרו מלאכי השרת לפני הקדוש ברוך הוא:
"רבון העולמים מה אתה מבזה תכסיס אלטיכסייה שלך?
תעלה אמת מן הארץ"
הדא הוא דכתיב "אמת מארץ תצמח"

Rabbi Simon says, "When G-d was about to create Adam, the angels on high divided into different camps. Some said he should not be created; others said he should be created.

Kindness said, 'Let him be created, for he will be generous and kind.'

Truth said, 'Do not create him for he will be full of lies.'

Righteousness said, 'Create him for he will do charity and righteousness.'

Peace said, 'Do not create him for he is full of conflict.'

So G-d took Truth and threw it to the ground, and then created man.

The angels on high said to G-d, 'Master of the Universe: how can you denigrate your seal [for G-d's seal is truth]?' The angels said, 'Let Truth rise from the earth.'

G-d accepted their words.

Thus it says in the book of Psalms: 'and truth will sprout from the earth (Tehillim/Psalms 85:11).' "

BEREISHIT RABAH, OP. CIT., 8:5

Key Points

1. At the heart of lying is duplicity, or the projecting of something other than that which is truly in one's heart or mind. Even where no malice is intended (such as in the cases of flattery, or lying to a child), the very act of lying is generally proscribed in Jewish tradition.

2. The fundamental rationale for the virtue of honesty is the mitzvah to emulate G-d the virtue of the essential divine quality is truth. Torah defines truth as that which is everlasting, a quality that ultimately describes only G-d; as such, it is the foundation of our world.

3. Truth benefits both society and the individual: lying undermines integrity, and tangles the liar in a debilitating web.

4. Torah, however, does not promote a slavish devotion to truth; as the essential feature of integrity, truth is better served in certain situations through being hidden.

5. Lying is permitted in selected contexts, such as maintaining peace, preserving modesty and privacy, preventing evil people from causing harm, or maintaining necessary optimism in a critically ill patient.

6. Truth is the elixir of life and therefore worth upholding to the greatest degree possible. Only in the times to come, however, will the world be sufficiently refined so that truth and peace can coexist in perfect harmony.

Additional Readings

Geneivat Da'at: The Prohibition Against Deception in Today's World

by **Hershey H. Friedman**

*Professor of Business and Marketing
Department of Economics
Brooklyn College of the City
University of New York*

The literal meaning of *geneivat da'at* in Hebrew is theft of one's mind, thoughts, wisdom, or knowledge, i.e., fooling someone and thereby causing him or her to have a mistaken assumption, belief, and/or impression. Thus, the term is used in Jewish law to indicate deception, cheating, creating a false impression, and acquiring undeserved goodwill. *Geneivat da'at* goes beyond lying. Any words or actions that cause others to form incorrect conclusions about one's motives might be a violation of this prohibition. One does not have the right to diminish the ability of another person, Jew or Gentile, to make a fair and honest evaluation, whether in business or interpersonal relations.

Many scholars (Ritva in the name of the Baalei Tosafos, Babylonian Talmud, Chullin 94a; Rabbi Eliezer of Metz, Sefer Yereim, Chapter 224) believe that the proscription against *geneivat da'at* is included in the transgression of "you shalt not steal (Leviticus 19:11)." In Leviticus, the commandment against stealing is in the plural, *lo tignovu* (in the Ten Commandments it is in the singular, *lo tignov*), which enables one to broaden the law to encompass more situations. Sforno asserts that the eighth of the Ten Commandments (Exodus 20:13), "Thou shalt not steal," while primarily referring to kidnapping, also includes stealing money and *geneivat da'at*. Rabbi Yonah Gerondi (Shaarei Teshuvah 3:184) regards *geneivat da'at* as a form of falsehood; the Torah explicitly states (Exodus 23:7) "Distance yourself from a false matter." Others, however, believe that the prohibition against *geneivat da'at* is not Biblical but rabbinical (Semak, 262).

The Talmudic View

The sages believed that there are seven types of thieves and, of these, the most egregious is the one who "steals the minds" of people (Tosefta Bava Kama 7:3). The Talmud (Babylonian Talmud, Chullin 94a-b) discusses the principle of *geneivat da'at*. "Shmuel states: It is forbidden to steal the mind of anyone, even idolaters." The Talmud then notes that Shmuel never expressly stated the above but it was deduced from an incident in which his attendant duped a heathen ferryman. There is a dispute in the Talmud as to what happened. One opinion is that Shmuel told his attendant to give the ferryman a chicken and the latter thought he was getting a kosher chicken but was actually given one that was unkosher. Another opinion is that the ferryman thought he was receiving undiluted wine but was instead given diluted wine.

Rabbi Meir (Babylonian Talmud, Chullin 94a) in further elaborating on the rules of *geneivat da'at*, states that a person should not urge his friend to dine with him knowing that he will refuse. One should not offer gifts to another person knowing that the latter will not accept them. One should not open a barrel of wine for someone making him believe that it was done for his honor when, in reality, the barrel was sold to a shopkeeper and was going to be opened anyway. It is permitted if he informs his guest of the arrangement. If one's oil jar is empty, one should not tell his guest to anoint himself with oil knowing that he will refuse anyway. The Talmud states, however, that in the above cases, if the purpose of the request is to show the guest honor, it is allowed. The cases cited by Rabbi Meir involve undeserved goodwill. For instance, repeatedly inviting a person to a meal knowing full well that he or she will refuse results in undeserved goodwill. The invitee will believe that s/he is special in the eyes of the inviter and may even feel an obligation to reciprocate. While this is not outright theft it is inappropriate behavior for a moral individual.

The Talmud (Babylonian Talmud, Chullin 94a) also states that one should not go to a mourner's house with a bottle of wine that is only partially full. Apparently, in Talmudic times, comforters would bring bottles of wine for the mourners. An individual could easily bring a bottle that was nearly empty and strategically place it among the other bottles in a way so that the mourners would assume that the reason the bottle was empty was that people had drunk from it (see Maharsha). Nor should one fill the partially empty wine bottle with water since he deceives the mourner. This is also a case of *geneivat da'at* since the mourner will think he is being given a full bottle of wine. The Talmud adds that if there is a big assembly of people at the mourner's house and the comforter wants to show respect for the mourner (but cannot afford to bring a full bottle of wine), he is permitted the above deception. Again, this case demonstrates that if the purpose of the *geneivat da'at* is not to receive undeserved gratitude but to show honor or pay tribute to another person, it is permitted.

It is clear that *geneivat da'at* applies even in situations in which there is no loss of money. If *geneivat da'at* in buying and selling results in a financial loss, the buyer then has recourse to the courts under the laws regarding *mekach taos* (transactions made in error) and possibly *ona'ah* (overcharge). However, even if there is no financial loss and even in interpersonal situations that do not involve money, one is still prohibited from deceiving another person. The Maharsha (Babylonian Talmud, Chullin 94a) discusses the Talmudic dictum that one should not sell shoes made from the hide of an animal that died and claim that it came from an animal that was slaughtered (the latter hide is stronger). He notes that the above misrepresentation would be a problem of *ona'ah* (overcharging), since the hides from a slaughtered animal are of better quality and cost more than hides from animals that died. He therefore explains the Talmud as referring to a case in which the shoes were sold at a fair price. The seller, however, misrepresented the transaction and told the buyer that the shoes were made from hide that was from a slaughtered animal. There is no *ona'ah* because the price is reasonable; however, the seller has earned undeserved gratitude from the buyer who believes that he has received a bargain. This is why sellers are obligated to reveal any defect in a product, even if they intend to sell the product at a fair price that takes the imperfection into account.

The Talmud (Tosefta, Baba Metzia 3: 15) states that a storekeeper is not permitted to sprinkle his store with wine or oil because he "steals the minds" of people. Several commentaries (e.g., Magen Abraham, Minchas Bikurim) feel that the problem with sprinkling one's store with a superior-quality, fragrant wine is that it may fool customers into believing that all the wine sold in the store is of the same high quality. People tend to rely on their sense of smell when purchasing products such as wine or oil.

There are some exceptions to the rule prohibiting *geneivat da'at*. Numerous commentaries (e.g., Bach, Me'irat Einayim, Be'er Ha'Golah) indicate that there is nothing wrong with inviting someone to a meal or party that he or she cannot attend if the intent is to be polite. The prohibition is against "urging" the other party, making numerous requests to attend, and thus appearing very eager to invite him/her. Since the inviter is aware that the invitee cannot attend, repeated requests produce undeserved goodwill. Asking only once or twice, on the other hand, is the accepted protocol and will not be misinterpreted by the invitee. Indeed, not asking someone to come to a party could result in hurt feelings; others may think the person was not invited because he is an unworthy individual.

The Talmud (Babylonian Talmud, Chullin 94b) indicates that *geneivat da'at* may not be an issue if an individual has deceived himself. Mar Zutra b. Nachman was traveling from the town of Sikara to Mahuza at the same time that Rava and Rabbi Safra were going to Mahuza. They met and Mar Zutra assumed that the two sages had come specifically to meet him, so he told them that they should not have gone to the trouble. Rabbi Safra felt obliged to explain to Mar Zutra that he had not known of his arrival, but had he known, he would have done even more. Rava, however, thought that this disclaimer was not necessary since Mar Zutra had deceived himself. Tosafos (Babylonian Talmud, Chullin 94b) makes a distinction between this case and the above case with the barrel of wine that was sold to a shopkeeper and was thus not being opened specifically for the guest. In the case of the barrel of wine, the logical expectation is that the barrel of wine is being opened for the guest. This is why the mistaken assumption has to be corrected. In the case of Mar Zutra, there is no reason to assume when encountering people traveling on a road that they have come to greet you. Thus, one is not obligated to correct the misimpression. Levine (2000, pp. 21-22, 38-39, 120-121) uses the logic of the hypothetical "reasonable man" and states (p. 120): "the seller's disclosure obligation consists not only of a duty not to mislead in an affirmative manner but also of a requirement to disabuse the customer of his reasonable misperception about the product." The obligation is to correct sensible and logical misunderstandings, not errors that reasonable and sensible people would not make.

The Shulchan Aruch

The *Shulchan Aruch*, written by Rabbi Yosef Caro, is accepted throughout the Jewish world as the authoritative work on *halacha* (Jewish law). It was completed in the middle of the 16th Century and means "set table." It lives up to its name and is easy-to-read, concise, and to the point. It is based to a large degree on Maimonides' classic legal code known as *Mishneh Torah* ("a repetition of the Torah"), which was completed between 1170 and 1180 CE. The *Shulchan Aruch* and the *Mishneh Torah* are two of the best-known Jewish legal codes.

The Shulchan Aruch (Choshen Mishpat, 228:6) states that one is not allowed to fool others in buying and selling or to "steal their minds." Thus, if there is a defect in merchandise, the seller is obligated to inform the buyer, even if the buyer is an idolater. One is also not permitted to sell meat of an animal that died (and is therefore not kosher) to an idolater and misrepresent it as ritually slaughtered meat and thus kosher. Although the idolater has not suffered any financial loss, he believes that the Jew cares for him by selling him meat that is permissible to Jews. This results in undeserved gratitude. The Shulchan Aruch then adds that one is not permitted to "steal the mind" of others with words (*geneivat da'at b'dvarim*) and make it appear as though he is doing something on his fellow's behalf if he does not intend to do it. Examples of this include the above-cited cases discussed by Rabbi Meir dealing with undeserved gratitude/goodwill (e.g., inviting someone to a feast, offering a gift to someone who will refuse it, and opening a barrel of wine). Maimonides also discusses *geneivat da'at* in the area of transactions (Mishneh Torah, Hilchot Mechirah 18:1) and in interpersonal relations (Mishneh Torah, Hilchot De'ot 2:6). As noted above, *geneivat da'at* has ramifications in both business transactions and personal interactions (e.g., insincere invitations).

The Shulchan Aruch (Choshen Mishpat, 228: 6-7) notes that the proscription against *geneivat da'at* does not apply in two situations: (1) If an individual should have realized that something was not necessarily being done for his benefit (as in the case involving Mar Zutra and the two sages) but mistakenly believed so, then one is not obligated to inform him of his erroneous assumption. (2) If one offers someone something knowing that he will refuse not because he seeks undeserved gratitude but because he wants to show honor and respect for the other party, then it is permitted.

Situations involving Geneivat Da'at

The following are some situations that may involve *geneivat da'at*. The purpose of this paper is not to arrive at definitive *halachic* (Jewish law) conclusions but to make the public aware of the issues involving *geneivat da'at*. Those who desire to know the final *halacha* should consult with a *halachic* authority.

Deceptive Offers: Urging someone to come to a meal knowing that s/he will not come; offering a person a gift knowing that he will not accept it; and opening a barrel of wine that one had to open anyway and make guests believe that it was opened strictly for them. These cases are directly from the Talmud (Babylonian Talmud, Chullin 94a). Modern versions of the above might include offering a person a lift home from a party knowing that she arrived with her own car and does not need a lift. Sending a wedding or bar mitzvah invitation to an individual that you know will not or cannot come should not be a problem if you are doing it to show respect to the invitee. Also, inviting someone to a party or wedding in order that his or her feelings are not hurt would be permissible. As noted above, the problem is with "urging" (i.e., making repeated requests) someone to come. Sending an invitation is also considered proper etiquette even if the inviter knows the invitee cannot make it. If, however, the invitation is sent for one's own benefit, e.g., to receive a gift, and the reality is that one does not want the person to come, there may be a problem of *geneivat da'at*. Making a gift appear much more valuable than it really is would also be prohibited by Jewish law (Basri 1982, p. 245).

Irregular Merchandise: Sellers are obligated to disclose any defects, deficiencies, shortcomings, or imperfections in their merchandise; otherwise, they are guilty of *geneivat da'at*. This is true even if the product is being sold at a fair price so that there is no problem of *mekach taos*. Tamari (1991, pp. 73-76) stresses that Jewish law rejects the concept of "Let the buyer beware;" the burden of ensuring that the buyer is not deceived is on the seller.

Deceptive Quality/Advertising Puffery: Misleading one's customers into thinking that the quality of the item they purchased is much better than it really is would be *geneivat da'at*. This case is similar to the Talmudic case (Babylonian Talmud, Chullin 94a) involving selling shoes made from the hide of a dead animal and misrepresenting them as coming from the hide of a slaughtered animal. Deceptive advertising would be one way of dishonestly raising customers' expectations regarding the quality of products. Selling products with misleading nutritional information, e.g., selling nutrition supplements as weight-loss, wrinkle-elimination, or memory-improvement aids when there is no evidence that they have any such beneficial effect, would also fall under the prohibition of *geneivat da'at*.

Spitz (1997) states that if individuals believe that the quality of a product manufactured in one place or country (e.g., Swiss watches, Japanese cameras) is superior to that of competing brands made elsewhere, then sellers are not permitted to suggest or hint that the merchandise comes from the area with the reputation for superior quality if this is not the case. Levine (1987, pp. 51-57) asserts that advertising puffery may also result in *geneivat da'at* and thus be prohibited by Jewish law. Puffery is exaggerated, overstated advertising; the kind on which reasonable consumers will generally not rely. Puffery might include very vague and/or subjective statements regarding product superiority, e.g., "best in the universe," "whiter than white," or "fit for an emperor." True puffery is not usually regarded as deceptive advertising. Levine, however, believes that if the puffery produces expectations on the part of the consumer that the product cannot deliver, then it would be considered *geneivat da'at*. Tamari (1996, p. 74) feels that deceptive packaging that makes customers believe that they are receiving larger or more items may also constitute *geneivat da'at*.

Levine (2000, pp. 60 -61) discusses a comparative advertisement for Baby Orajel, a product that helps alleviate the pain of teething babies that notes that the product works within one minute, whereas Children's Tylenol takes up to 30 minutes to take effect. The advertisement states: "If you're giving your baby Children's Tylenol, your baby could wind up suffering up to thirty minutes longer than necessary." What the advertisement does not state is that Baby Orajel wears off much sooner than Tylenol. This, according to Levine, constitutes *geneivat da'at*.

Deceptive Bargains: Deceiving one's customers and making them believe that they have received a bargain when they have not would also be *geneivat da'at*. Thus, phony markdowns, i.e., marking an item with a spurious high price solely for the purpose of slashing it and thus make customers think they are getting a bargain is prohibited. In addition, falsely claiming "last day of sale" would also be forbidden [Tamari (1996), p. 74].

Levine (1987, p. 48) states that firms that find that they are stuck with a product that is not selling well and therefore have to reduce the price to eliminate the excess inventory are not permitted to promote the sale as a discount sale and thereby suggest that customers are obtaining a bargain. Since, in reality, the price discount is due to declining demand, the new price represents a "fair" price, not a bargain price, and the firm should call the "sale" a clearance sale. Otherwise, the firm would acquire undeserved goodwill. Tamari (1991, pp. 75-76) notes that advertisements claiming sale prices that are in actuality not lower than the regular price are *geneivat da'at*. Kaufman (2002, p. 39) prohibits a firm from running advertisements that state "Watches normally $39.99, now only $19.99" if the $39.99 price is simply the manufacturer's suggested selling price, not the usual selling price for these watches. Spitz (2001) maintains that retailers may not claim the following if they are untrue: "I can give it to you for $50, but not less, because that's what I myself paid for it"; "This is the best model of its kind"; and "the cheapest prices in town." It is clear from the above opinions that a seller is not permitted to make a buyer believe that she has obtained a bargain when the reality is that she has paid the regular price. Even causing a customer to believe that they have received an "exceptional bargain" when all they have gotten is a small bargain would be problematic.

Deceptive Credentials/Cheating on Examinations: Cheating on examinations is definitely a violation of *geneivat da'at*. Both the teacher of the course and future employers who rely on grades to determine the abilities of potential employees have been deceived. Rabbi Moshe Feinstein (Igros Moshe, Choshen Mishpat 2: 30) and Rabbi Menashe Klein (Mishna Halacha 7: 275) make it clear that cheating on tests given in secular studies is prohibited. Additional information on this subject may be found at Povarsky (1995) and Resnicoff (2002).

Similar to the problem of cheating on examinations, is the question of the permissibility of changing the details of cases discussed in a medical paper to make the article more publishable and thus improve one's chances of getting a job. In various fields such as academe, a resume containing several publications is more likely to lead to a job than one with few publications. Rabbi Waldenberg (Tsits Eliezer, vol. 15, no. 12) felt that this also falls under the prohibition of *geneivat da'at*. It is interesting to note that Nuovo (2002) recently published a paper that discussed the problem of the use of statistics in medical studies to make new drugs sound much more effective than the reality.

Levine (2000, p. 330) indicates that "creating a false impression for the purpose of counteracting an unwarranted bias" may be permitted under some circumstances. Thus, one may be permitted to dye his beard to make himself or herself appear younger and thereby get a job. This, however, is only permitted if the individual is young enough to perform the required work. Suppose the work involves, say, heavy lifting that is more appropriate for a much younger person, then dying one's hair and beard to appear youthful would not be permissible.

Deceptive Testimonials: Product testimonials and endorsements may be problematic according to Levine (1987, pp. 57-59). Since in most cases experts and testing laboratories that endorse products are paid for their services, they are not unbiased. If the public believes that their opinions are truly objective and impartial, the endorsement will constitute *geneivat da'at*.

Deceptive Accounting Practices: Accountants or auditors who purposely provide deceptive financial statements are guilty of *geneivat da'at* (Tamari (1995),

pp. 65-66). Needless to say, the recent scandals involving Enron, Global Crossing, Tyco, WorldCom, Adelphia Communications, Rite Aid, and several other firms demonstrate how easy it is for auditors to use creative accounting to distort the true financial situation of a company and deceive the public. Friedman (2002) notes that dishonest auditors are also guilty of *lifnei iver*, placing a "stumbling block before a blind person."

Deception for Charity: If an individual, even an idolater, requests that his or her contribution be given to a specific charity, switching to another charity without the consent of the donor would be *geneivat da'at* (Rashi, Babylonian Talmud, Baba Bathra 11a).

In many synagogues the custom is to auction off various honors, e.g., being called up to the Torah, and the proceeds usually go to the synagogue. Suppose one knows that an individual will pay anything to get a particular honor, say, getting called up to the Torah on Yom Kippur, is it permissible to bid against the individual in order to drive up the price and thus benefit the synagogue? This question is discussed in *Sheilot U'Teshuvot Yosef Ometz* (Section 57) and in the case discussed there is an additional factor. The shill has agreed that if he wins the bidding war, that he will only have to pay a fraction of what he bid. According to *Yosef Ometz*, this is prohibited and is *geneivat da'at*. First, if the shill wins the bidding war and obtains the honor, the other members of the synagogue will think he donated a great deal to the synagogue for the honor when the reality is that he contributed considerably less. Second, even if the shill loses the bidding war, the members of the congregation will think that he was willing to donate a considerable amount, when, in reality, he had no interest in giving that large an amount to the synagogue.

Conclusion

Certainly, we all should strive to be as straightforward and honest as possible in all our dealings, not only business. Indeed, the Talmud (Jerusalem Talmud, Makkot 2:6) declares that if an individual is knowledgeable in one tractate of the Talmud and he goes to another town in which people want to provide him with honor because they believe that he knows two tractates, he is required to correct their false impression. This seems to contradict the Babylonian Talmud (Chullin 94b) that indicates that if people have fooled themselves, one is not obligated to correct the misperception. However, in this case it is not unreasonable to expect that one who has expertise in one tractate also has proficiency in another since many of the tractates of the Talmud are interrelated, interconnected, and overlapping (Levine 2000, p. 120-121). In addition, the individual is actually being honored for his accomplishments in two tractates and his participation strengthens this false belief (Spitz, 1997). The prohibition against *geneivat da'at*, as noted above, goes beyond simply requiring that one not deceive. Individuals must correct false impressions that have been made by other people making reasonable assumptions as to one's motives both in business and non-business situations.

Geneivat da'at is not a minor prohibition. Rabbi Eliezer of Metz (Sefer Yereim 224) says that Absalom, son of King David, deserved death for violating the Torah law against *geneivat da'at*. As the Talmud notes (Babylonian Talmud, Sotah 9b), Absalom "stole the hearts" (Rabbi Metz clearly believes that "stealing the heart" is the same as *geneivat da'at*) of three parties - his father, the court, and the people of Israel - and therefore was punished in that his heart was pierced by three darts (II Samuel 18:14).

References

Basri, Ezra (1982). *Dinei Memonot*. Part Four. Jerusalem: Haktav Institute.

Friedman, Hershey H. (2002). "Placing a Stumbling Block Before the Blind Person: An In-Depth Analysis." *Jewish Law Articles*, http://www.jlaw.com/Articles/placingstumbling.html, (June 2002).

Kaufman, Moshe H. (2002). *Money: The Bottom Line*. Jerusalem: Feldheim Publishers.

Levine, Aaron (1987). *Economics and Jewish Law*. New York: Yeshiva University Press/Ktav Publishing House.

_____ (2000). *Case Studies in Jewish Business Ethics*. New York: Yeshiva University Press/Ktav Publishing House.

Nuovo, Jim, Joy Melnikow, and Denise Chang (2002). "Reporting Number Needed to Treat and Absolute Risk Reduction in Randomized Controlled Trials." *Journal of the American Medical Association*, Vol. 287 (21), June 5, 2813-2814.

Povarsky, Chaim (1995). "Responsa Literature on Contemporary Issues: Cheating on Tests." *Jewish Law Report, Touro College*, http://www.tourolaw.edu/publications/jewishlaw/apr95/, (June 2002).

Resnicoff, Steven (2002). "A Jewish View on Cheating." *Jewish Law Commentary*, http://www.jlaw.com/Commentary/cheatinginschool.html, (June 2002).

Spitz, Tzvi (1997). "Geneivas Da'as: Misleading Others." *Advanced Business Halacha-Torah.Org*, http://torah.org/advanced/business-halacha/5757/vol2no30.html, (June 2002).

_____ (2001). *Cases in Monetary Halachah*. Brooklyn, NY: Mesorah Publications, Ltd.

Tamari, Meir (1991). *In the Marketplace*. Southfield, Michigan: Targum Press.

_____ (1995). *The Challenge of Wealth*. Northvale, NJ: Jason Aronson, Inc.

_____ (1996). *Al Chet: Sins in the Marketplace*. Northvale, NJ: Jason Aronson, Inc.

http://www.jlaw.com/Articles/geneivatdaat.html

Reprinted with permission from JLaw.com

Should Moral Individuals Ever Lie?
Insights from Jewish Law

by **Hershey H. Friedman, Ph.D.**
and **Abraham C. Weisel, Esq.**© 2003 Dr.
H. H. Friedman and A. C. Weisel

Abstract

Dishonesty and deception are serious crimes in Jewish law. The Torah explicitly demands that one should "Distance himself from a false matter." There are, however, situations in which Jewish law permits or even demands that one engage in deception. This paper will discuss when it is permissible in Jewish law to prevaricate and deceive.

Recently, a psychology study found that the average person lies about 150 to 200 times per day. (Geary, 2000; Walsh, 2001). At first blush, such numbers seem to stagger rather than inform. Most people would be offended if they were told that they tell an average of eight to twelve untruths every waking hour. Nonetheless, after additional reflection and careful consideration of true day-to-day social interactions, we almost intuit that lying is not only more common than we expect, it is more necessary as well.

Indubitably, truth is important for the welfare of society. The famous dictum by Rabbi Shimon ben Gamliel (Babylonian Talmud, Avot 1:18) proclaims "the world endures on three things: justice, truth, and peace." It is difficult to imagine a society surviving for long if no one cares about honesty. Are there situations where one is permitted, or even obligated, to lie? This is a question that has been of great interest to theologians, philosophers, and religious leaders.

It appears that Aristotle in his *Ethics* feels that it is never permissible to prevaricate. Plato, on the other hand, in his *Republic*, is of the opinion that there are situations when one is indeed permitted to lie. For instance, he allows physicians to lie to patients if it is for their own good and statesmen to deceive if it is for the welfare of the public. Similarly, Christian thinkers and modern philosophers have also divided into two camps: Those who take an absolutist position on lying, whereby it is always forbidden, and those who believe that falsehoods are sometimes necessary, and accordingly, permissible.

In *De Mendacio* (On Lying), written c. 395 C.E., Augustine takes an absolutist approach to lying. Citing Psalms (5:6-7) he rhetorically queries: How can one ever prevaricate if the Lord abhors liars and will destroy them? Accordingly, Augustine does not agree with those that favorably point to the two Hebrew midwives, Shifrah and Puah, who risked their lives by lying to the Pharaoh in order to save the newborn Israelite babies in Egypt (Exodus 1:19-21), as proof that it may be praiseworthy to be dishonest. To Augustine, lies are abhorrent, even if for a good purpose. Augustine, however, espouses a hierarchy among eight types of lies, ranging from falsehoods "in religious doctrine" (the worst) to lies that do not hurt anyone. Similarly, Thomas Aquinas (*Summa Theologia*, Part II, Question 110) also took an absolutist approach to lying and believed that "every lie is a sin" yet he too, makes distinctions among falsehoods. Jocose (made in jest) and officious (for the benefit of others) lies are not mortal sins and "the greater the good intended, the more is the sin of lying diminished in gravity." Unsurprisingly, injurious, hurtful lies that are harmful to others are deemed mortal sins.

Immanuel Kant also took the absolutist position and claimed that a lie is a "crime of man against his own person" and must therefore be shunned regardless of the costs. He also took the position that one is never permitted to lie even if there is a murderer at the door looking for his victim's room.

Some religious leaders did not agree with the absolutist view on falsehoods. St. John Chrysostom believed that lying in order to benefit others is permitted. Cassian and Origen felt that sometimes lies are necessary but they should be used the way we use medicine, something we do with distaste but out of necessity (Catholic Encyclopedia). Martin Luther also felt that lying for the sake of the Christian church would not be a sin.

Grotius (tr. 1925), the seventeenth century Dutch theologian and legal scholar, by many considered "the father of modern international law," also rejects the absolutist position and asserts that falsehoods are only a problem if it violates the right of the individual who hears it. Suppose the individual telling the lie has wicked intentions, then s/he forfeits the right to hear the truth. Similarly, children are too young to have acquired this right and thus may be lied to.

Sidgwick (1966, 313-316) makes the argument that if we may kill to defend ourselves, why should we not be able to lie if this will provide us with a better means of protection? He asserts the following:

Where deception is designed to benefit the person deceived, Common Sense seems to concede that it may sometimes be right: for example, most persons would not hesitate to speak falsely to an invalid, if this seemed the only way of concealing facts that might produce a dangerous shock: nor do I perceive that any one shrinks front telling fictions to children, on matters upon which it is thought well that they should not know the truth.

Bok (1999; pp. 90 -106) feels that there are several conditions that may excuse a falsehood. A "test of publicity" should be used to determine whether a lie is justifiable. The test asks (p. 93): "Which lies, if any, would survive the appeal for justification to reasonable persons? It requires us to seek concrete and open performance of an exercise crucial to ethics: the Golden Rule, basic to so many religious and moral traditions."

Bok suggests that, as part of the test, one should first consult with her own conscience and ask how she would feel if roles were reversed and she were lied to. Also, will this lie encourage others to lie or even change the personality of the individual who has been untruthful so that she now finds it easy to lie, even when it is not justifiable? After introspection, one should consult with a small but representative group of people to see how they feel about the lie and would they approve of it. Clearly, lying to the murderer looking for his victim or to the Gestapo seeking Jews in hiding would easily pass the "test of publicity" and would be permissible.

According to Nietzsche, "lying is a necessity of life." Stiegnitz contends that lying starts with "how are you?" a question for which no one really cares to hear the answer. Stiegnitz believes that telling falsehoods are "an essential part of survival in everyday life" and "as necessary to life as air and water" (Geary, 2000; Walsh, 2001). Nyberg (1993) also believes that without lying, it would be virtually impossible to have a relationship. Society could not survive if we all felt compelled to always tell the truth.

Intuitively, it appears obvious that truth can be quite hurtful. Some secular writers seem to align themselves with the anti-absolutist position:

"A truth that's told with bad intent
Beats all the lies you can invent." [William Blake]

"Tis not enough your counsel still be true;
Blunt truths more mischief than nice falsehoods do."
[Alexander Pope]

"The truth is an awful weapon of aggression.
It is possible to lie, and even to murder, with the truth."
[Alfred Adler]

The Jewish View on Lying

The Torah seems to be unequivocal with regard to lying: "Thou shall not bear false witness" (Exodus 20:16), "Thou shall not steal, thou shall not deny falsely, and thou shall not lie one to another" (Leviticus 19: 11), and "Distance yourself from a false matter" (Exodus 23:7). The first verse clearly applies to witnesses in a court; the second has been defined as a prohibition against swearing in order to avoid returning someone else's property (see Sefer HaChinuch 226). A closer perusal of the latter verse reveals that the Torah is regulating in the context of a Jewish court of law. As such, there is much dispute as to whether the proscription of lying in a non-judicial context is Biblically or Rabbinically based. Some halachic deciders are of the opinion that the Torah only explicitly forbids lying by judges and witnesses, whereas others apply this prohibition universally. For the former, the prohibition against lying to cause another financial harm derives from the verse (Leviticus 19: 36): "You shall have just scales, just weights, a just ephah (a dry measure), and a just *hin* (a liquid measure)." The Rabbis homiletically (Babylonian Talmud, Baba Metzia 49a) translate *hin* to mean "yes" based on the similarity of the word *hin* to the Aramaic word meaning yes (*hen*). According to the Talmud, the verse "a just *hin*" teaches us that an individual's "yes" should be just as should be his "no."

As far as lying in situations where no harm results, there is a dispute among the commentaries as to whether it is prohibited by the Torah. Yabrov (2000, pp.1-5) provides an extensive treatment and concludes that the majority of deciders are of the opinion that the verse "Distance yourself from a false matter" includes all kind of lies. We shall see, however, that the Talmud does not take an absolutist position on lying and permits and even encourages lying in certain situations.

There are four important Talmudic texts that deal with the issue of permissible deceptions. The first is the following (Babylonian Talmud, Yebamoth 65b).

Rabbi Ille'a said in the name of Rabbi Elazar son of Rabbi Shimon: It is permitted for a person to deviate from the truth in the interest of peace, as it says (Genesis 50:16-17): "Your father [Jacob] commanded before his death, saying: So shall you say to Joseph, 'O Please forgive the offense of your brothers and their sin for they have treated you so wickedly.'"

Rabbi Nathan said it is a commandment [to deviate from the truth in the interest of peace], as it says (I Samuel 16:2): "And Samuel said, 'How can I go? If Saul hears of it, he will kill me.'"

At the Academy of Rabbi Yishmael it was taught: Great is the cause of peace, seeing that for its sake, even the Holy One, blessed be He, changed the truth, for at first it is written (Genesis 18:12), 'My lord [i.e., husband Abraham] is old, while afterward it is written (18:13), "And I am old."

The case dealing with Joseph's brothers is as follows. After Jacob's death, Joseph's brothers feared that Joseph would retaliate against them and get even for what they had done to him. They therefore fabricated a story that Jacob begged Joseph to forgive his brothers for having sold him into slavery. There is no record of such an instruction and the Talmud assumes that the brothers invented the story in the name of peace.

The second case is where God Himself suggests to the prophet Samuel to bring a heifer and say that he came to sacrifice it, though the prophet's true mission was to anoint David as a successor for King Saul. The commentaries note that even though Samuel did indeed bring a sacrifice, the deception was in implying that this was the only purpose of his trip to Bethlehem.

Rabbi Yishmael's proof is from the story of Abraham and Sarah. When Sarah overheard one of the three "guests" telling Abraham that she would have a son by the following year she laughed and said to herself that her husband was old. God gets angry and asks Abraham why Sarah laughed in disbelief saying <u>she</u> was old, i.e., too old to have children. Seemingly, God altered the truth in order to spare Abraham's feelings.

It should be noted that Rabbi Nathan not only agrees that one is permitted to lie in the name of peace, he believes that it is a mitzvah (commandment) to lie if this will bring peace.

It appears that normative halacha agrees with the ruling of Rabbi Nathan [Yabrov 2000, p. 23].

The second text (Babylonian Talmud, Kethuboth 16b-17a) discusses the problem of what praises to say before a bride at her wedding.

The Rabbis taught: How does one dance before the bride [i.e., what does one say in praise of her]? The School of Shammai says: We praise the bride as she is. The School of Hillel says: We say that she is a beautiful and graceful bride. The School of Shammai said to the School of Hillel: If she was lame or blind, does one say about her that she is a beautiful and graceful bride? But the Torah said (Exodus 23: 7): "Distance yourself from a false matter." The School of Hillel said to the School of Shammai: According to your opinion, if someone made an inferior purchase in the marketplace, should one praise it or deprecate it in his eyes. Surely, one should praise it. From here [the latter statement of the Hillel School] the Sages said: A person's disposition should always be pleasant with people.

Tosafos notes that the School of Shammai agrees that if someone makes a bad purchase, others should laud the item. However, in the case of a bride, the sages should not institute a general rule that forces everyone to lie, given the Torah's aversion of falsehoods. Rabbi Isaiah diTrani (Tosefot RI"D) also notes that the opinion of the Sages is that one has to be pleasant with people even if it means that he has to lie. The Ritva (Rabbi Yomtov ben Abraham), in his discussion of the above Talmudic passage, states in an unambiguous manner that wherever one has to be concerned about "the ways of peace" there is no prohibition of "Distance yourself from a false matter." This would probably include such statements as "you look good," "nice to see you," "thanks for the wonderful gift," "I really had a wonderful time," "You haven't aged a bit," or "I missed you." Being told by friends that "You look terrible," "I couldn't care less whether I saw you," "I hate your gift," "I had a lousy time," "Boy, did you age," or "I did not miss you at all" would not further the cause of peace.

The above passage regarding "how one dances before the bride" also appears in another tractate of the Talmud (Babylonian Talmud, Kallah Rabbathi 10). There, however, the Talmud notes that the School of Hillel connects the proscription (Exodus 23:7) of "Distance yourself from a false matter" with the end of the verse that states "And the innocent and righteous do not slay." The verse, therefore, is speaking of testifying falsely and thereby causing an innocent person to be executed. The Talmud concludes that the Hillel School believes that when the lie preserves life, e.g., strengthening the bond between bride and groom, lying is acceptable.

The third text (Babylonian Talmud, Bava Metzia 23b-24a) describes three situations when even scholars may lie.

Rabbi Yehuda stated in the name of Shmuel: In the following three matters it is the practice of the rabbis not to tell the truth: In matters of a tractate, a bed, and hospitality.

If a rabbi is asked whether he is familiar with a certain tractate, he may, for the sake of humility, answer in the negative even if he is knowledgeable in that tractate. Of course, one should not disclaim knowledge of a particular tractate if one asks because he seeks help. According to Rashi, the meaning of "bed" is that if a rabbi is asked whether he engaged in sexual relations with his wife, he may, for the sake of modesty, answer that he has not. Tosafos does not accept this explanation since people do not normally ask someone whether or not he slept with his wife. Tosafos offers an alternative explanation. One may lie if he was asked whether or not he slept in a particular bed. The bed may be stained from an emission and this could be embarrassing. "Hospitality" refers to a situation where one is asked whether a host was hospitable or not. If one is too effusive in his praise, especially

in front of ne'er-do-wells, he may cause problems for his host. It is therefore better to lie and downplay how good his host was.

The fourth case (Babylonian Talmud, Nedarim 27b) describes where lies to thieves are permitted in order to protect oneself from financial harm.

One is permitted to make a vow to murderers, plunderers, and [corrupt] tax collectors that the produce they wish to seize is *terumah* [which is only permitted to be eaten by priests and therefore of little value; an alternative explanation is that even murderers and robbers would not violate the prohibition against using *terumah*], even if it is not *terumah*, or that the property they wish to seize belongs to the Royal House, even if it does not.

We have a situation where one is dealing with immoral people and the victim has no other recourse. It should be noted that the dishonest tax collector discussed in the Talmud is an individual who pays the ruler a fee for the right to collect taxes, and then imposes exorbitant and inequitable taxes (the Talmud refers to this as "taxes without a limit") on the public. In a similar vein, later in the same tractate, (Babylonian Talmud, Nedarim 62b), Rava relates that a Torah scholar is permitted to declare that he is a "servant of fire" in order to evade paying communal taxes — the pagan priests of the fire-worshippers were exempt from taxes. The two justifications given by the commentaries are: (1) it is clear that the purpose of this declaration is to avoid a tax and not to suggest that one is renouncing his belief in God; (2) the term "servant of fire" could refer to God who is compared in the Torah (Deuteronomy 4:24) to a "consuming fire." Moreover, the Ran explains that this law applies to every Jew and is not limited to Torah scholars.

Thus, there are several circumstances where one is permitted or sometimes required to lie:

• Lying to preserve the cause of peace, not to hurt another person's feelings, or to provide comfort.

• Lying in a situation where honesty might cause oneself or another person harm.

• Lying for the sake of modesty or in order not to appear arrogant.

• Lying for the sake of decency, i.e., not telling the truth about intimate matters.

• Lying to protect one's property from scoundrels.

Lying to Preserve the Cause of Peace or in Order Not to Hurt Another Person's Feelings

Aaron the High Priest, brother of Moses, was known in Talmudic and Midrashic literature as a lover of peace. The following passage indicates that one may use deception in order to bring peace between people who are quarreling (Babylonian Talmud, Avot D'Rabbi Nathan 12: 3; Babylonian Talmud, Perek Hashalom).

When two people had a dispute, Aaron [the High Priest] went and sat near one of them and said to him: "My son, see what your friend is doing? He is beating his heart and tearing his clothing saying: "Woe is me. How can I lift up my eyes and look at my friend. I am ashamed of myself since I was the one who offended him." Aaron would sit with him until he removed the hatred from his heart. Aaron would then go and sit next to the other and say to him: "My son, see what your friend is doing? He is beating his heart and tearing his clothing saying: "Woe is me. How can I lift up my eyes and look at my friend. I am ashamed of myself since I was the one who offended him." Aaron would sit with him until he removed the hatred from his heart.

When the two met, they hugged and kissed each other.

The above story about Aaron makes it quite apparent that Jewish law recognizes that lying to bring peace is a commandment. Indeed, Aaron is praised in the Talmud as the lover and pursuer of peace (Babylonian Talmud, Avot 1:12).

The Talmud and Midrash (Jerusalem Talmud, Sotah 1:4; Midrash Leviticus Rabbah 9:9) relate that a certain woman was wont to attend the lectures given by Rabbi Meir. One evening, the lecture ended late, and upon arriving home, the woman's husband vowed to her that she would not be permitted to reenter his house until she spat in the face of the lecturer. Upon hearing of the woman's dilemma, Rabbi Meir devised a ruse whereby he pretended to be afflicted by an eye ailment that necessitated someone spit in his eye. After she spat in his eye seven times, Rabbi Meir told her to return to her husband and tell him that she had bested his requirement by spitting in the lecturer's eye seven times, not just once.

The patriarch Jacob dissembled when he pretended not to believe Joseph's dream and even rebuked Joseph and said to him (Genesis 37:10): "What kind of dream is this that you have dreamt! Shall we come — I, your mother, and your brothers — to bow down to you on the ground?" Rashi notes that Jacob did this in order to "remove the jealousy from the heart of the brothers." It appears that Jacob was not entirely honest with Joseph's brothers in order to preserve the peace. Unfortunately, the ruse did not help since the next verse notes: "His brothers envied him; while his father kept the matter in his mind."

Judah prevaricated when he said to the Viceroy of Egypt, who was actually Joseph, (Genesis 44:20): "and his brother [Joseph] is dead." Judah was the one who, 22 years earlier, convinced his brothers to sell Joseph as a slave. Rashi and other commentaries feel that Judah lied because he was afraid that he would be asked to produce Joseph if he had said that he was alive. However, a Midrash (quoted in Torah Shleimah, Genesis 44:20) notes that Judah lied in the interest of peace. We assume that this refers to the possibility that the truth would cause additional problems for the family, i.e., Benjamin would have to remain a slave until Joseph is produced.

The Talmud (Babylonian Talmud, Eruvin 53b) relates that Rabbi Yehoshua once stayed at a certain inn. The hostess served beans on the first and second day and he ate them. On the third day, she burned the beans and he did not eat them. When she asked him why he did not eat the beans, he politely told her that he had already eaten during the daytime. This story also demonstrates that in order to spare the feelings of another person, it is permissible to tell a falsehood.

There is evidence that even Heaven uses deception in order to protect the feelings of others. The Talmud (Babylonian Talmud, Berachos 28a) relates that when

Rabbi Gamliel was the *Nasi* [President of the Sanhedrin], a proclamation was issued that "any scholar whose inside is not as his outside" [i.e., of perfect character] may not enter the house of study. This proclamation was nullified when Rabbi Elazar ben Azariah became the *Nasi*; the Talmud notes that either 400 or 700 benches had to be added to the academy. Rabbi Gamliel felt bad about this and was afraid that he was responsible for withholding Torah from good students. He was subsequently shown in a dream white casks full of ashes, indicating that the new students were not worthwhile. The Talmud concludes that this was not the case and the students were actually of high caliber. Evidently, Heaven did this to spare Rabbi Gamliel's feelings.

Fish (1981, pp. 62-63) cites numerous sources that state that one may lie in order to comfort another person. One proof he cites is from the Talmud (Babylonian Talmud, Nedarim 50a). There the story is told of how impoverished Rabbi Akiva and his wife, the daughter of the wealthy Kalba Sevuah, were. Kalba Sevuah disinherited his daughter when he heard that she was going to marry the poor, ignorant shepherd, Akiva. They were so impecunious that they had to sleep on straw. Elijah the Prophet disguised himself as a mortal and pretended to need straw for his wife who had given birth. Rashi and the Ran both note that Elijah did this in order to comfort them and make them realize there were people in the world in greater poverty.

Rabbi Meir's two sons died on the Sabbath. Beruriah, wife of Rabbi Meir, lied to her husband when he asked where they were, and said the two boys were at the house of study. She waited until he made *Havdalah*, the prayer signaling the end of the Sabbath, and had to deceive a second time about his sons' whereabouts. After Rabbi Meir ate something she broke the news to him very gently by comparing their children's lives to an object deposited with someone for safekeeping. The owner took back what belonged to him. She concluded by citing the verse (Job 1:21): "The Lord has given, the Lord has taken, May the name of the Lord be blessed (Midrash Yalkut Shimoni, Proverbs 31). Apparently, Beruriah did what was proper since the Midrash refers to her as "a capable wife" and relates this story in that regard.

The Talmud (Babylonian Talmud, Sanhedrin 11a) enumerates several stories where someone prevaricated in order to prevent the humiliation of another person. For instance, once Rabbi Gamliel asked that seven scholars join him the following morning in the upper chamber for the purpose of intercalating the year [i.e., proclaiming a leap year]. The next morning, they noticed that there was an extra person there. Rabbi Gamliel asked: "Who is the one who came up without permission?" Jewish law mandates that the year may be intercalated only by a court whose members were specifically designated for that purpose the previous evening. Rabbi Shmuel Hakatan arose and declared: "It was I who came up without permission. My purpose was not to participate in the intercalation, but to learn how the law is applied in practice." The Talmud states that Rabbi Shmuel Hakatan was actually invited to join in the intercalation, but stated a falsehood in order not to cause embarrassment for the intruder.

Something similar happened when Rebbi was delivering a lecture and the strong odor of garlic caused a disturbance. Rebbi said: "Let the person who has eaten the garlic, please leave." Rabbi Chiya arose and left; then all the disciples arose and left. Again, it turned out that Rabbi Chiya had not eaten garlic, but left in order not to shame the true perpetrator.

The Talmud (Babylonian Talmud, Sanhedrin 11a) relates another story in the same vein. To understand this story one must know how marriage worked in Talmudic times. In those days, the first stage of marriage known as *erusin* was followed a year later by the final stage known as *nesuin*. *Erusin*, could technically be done via cohabitation, but this method was strongly frowned upon. A woman appeared at the academy of Rabbi Meir and said that one of the students betrothed her [i.e., *erusin*] by cohabitation. Apparently, the woman did not remember which of the students betrothed her. The woman wanted the student to either complete the marriage [*nesuin*] or give her a divorce. Even though Rabbi Meir was not the guilty one, he gave her a bill of divorce and then all of the students gave her one as well.

Shechaniah also told an untruth in order not to embarrass others. Shechaniah told Ezra (Ezra 10:2): "We have trespassed against our God and have married foreign women of the peoples of the land." Shechaniah included himself in the sin of intermarrying with pagan women living in Judea. Actually, he had not committed the misdeed of intermarriage but included himself in order not to embarrass the others who had.

Fish (1981, p. 199) uses the famous story of how Rabbi Shimon ben Shetach (Jerusalem Talmud, Chagiga 2:2; Rashi, Babylonian Talmud, Sanhedrin 44b) captured 80 sorceresses who lived in Ashkelon and brought them to trial as evidence that one may lie to eradicate evil. In the story, Rabbi Shimon had 80 of his students hide dry clothing in a jar. During a downpour, he went with them to the cave where the sorceresses lived and had the young men hide nearby. Rabbi Shimon entered the cave and told them that he was a sorcerer who had the power to make 80 young people magically appear in dry clothing, despite the strong rain. Arguably, eradicating evil is another way of bringing peace to the world.

Lying in A Situation Where Honesty Might Cause Oneself or Another Person Physical Harm

Abraham asked his wife Sarah to lie and say that she was his sister because he was traveling with her to ancient Egypt, a place known for its lack of morality (Genesis 12:10-13). Ramban believes that Abraham unintentionally committed a "great sin" and endangered his wife's virtue because he should have had faith that God would save him and his family. After all, it was God who told Abraham to leave the land of his birthplace. However, even the Ramban would have to agree that, where one does not have the personal assurance of God, one should be permitted to lie. In fact, Abraham used the same ruse again when sojourning in Gerar (Genesis 20: 1-3). Isaac also uses the same lie when traveling in lands where the morality of the inhabitants is questionable and claims that his wife Rebeccah is his sister (Genesis 26: 7).

According to the Midrash (Midrash Tanchuma, Lech Lecha 5), Abraham hid Sarah in a locked box when traveling to Egypt. When the Egyptian customs officials asked him what was in the box, he tried to convince them that it contained barley. When the officials did not believe him and said that it might contain wheat, Abraham offered to pay the tax on wheat. The officials then claimed that it might contain pepper, so Abraham offered to pay the tax on pepper. They then claimed that it might contain gold. Eventually, they opened the box and found Sarah.

This Midrash also demonstrates that lying is permitted in order to protect someone from harm (Fish, p. 110).

The two midwives in Egypt, Shifra and Puah, undoubtedly did the right thing by lying to Pharaoh and thereby not take part in the attempt to murder newborns. There is no question that Jewish law obligates one to prevaricate in order to save one's own life or the life of another person. Rahab the harlot prevaricated in order to save the life of the two Jewish spies sent by Joshua to Jericho (see Joshua 2). The Midrash (Pirka D'Rabeinu Hakodosh 15) notes that Rahab told a lie yet inherited life in this world and in the world to come. In fact, eight prophets descended from her (Babylonian Talmud, Megilla 14b).

The following involves a deception over a remedy (Babylonian Talmud, Avodah Zarah 28a) and deals with a considerably more complex ethical situation.

Rabbi Yochanan suffered from *tzafdina* [a dangerous disease of the gums or teeth] and went to a certain heathen lady who made a remedy for him to use on Thursday and Friday. He said to her: "What should I do tomorrow [the Sabbath]"? She replied: "You will not need the treatment." Rabbi Yochanan said: "But what if I do need it?" She replied: "Swear to me that you will not reveal the remedy to anyone." Rabbi Yochanan swore to her: "To the God of Israel I will not reveal it." She then disclosed the remedy to him and the next day he taught it in his public lecture.

The Talmud asks: But did he not swear to her not to reveal it? The Talmud answers: He swore that he would not reveal it to the God of Israel, but to His people, Israel, he would reveal it. The Talmud asks: But is this not a profanation of the name of God? [when a Jew commits a misdeed, especially something as serious as swearing falsely, it causes people to denigrate Judaism and the Torah]. The Talmud answers that from the beginning he revealed to her that his oath was not binding [and that he wanted to help the public].

The above story is problematic since deception (*geneivat da'at*) is prohibited, even with an idolater. The loophole that Rabbi Yochanan employed does not take away from the fact that he deceived her. I believe the answer to this question is that to save a life, even one's own life, one is permitted to lie. *Tzafdina* was a deadly disease and

Rabbi Yochanan wanted to save the lives of many people who were afflicted with this malady. It is interesting to note that the above story is also told in the Jerusalem Talmud. There the Talmud has two opinions as to what happened to the heathen woman. One opinion was that she committed suicide. Another opinion was that she converted to Judaism presumably because she was impressed with Rabbi Yochanan's decision to go public with the cure rather than trying to enrich himself by selling the remedy. Rabbi Akiva (Babylonian Talmud, Kallah Rabbathi 2) used Rabbi Yochanan's approach to deceive a Jewish woman. He was trying to determine the status of her son who impudently uncovered his head in front of the sages.

In a converse situation, Shmuel (Babylonian Talmud, Shabbos 129a) deceived Ablat, a pagan, because he did not want him to learn about the value of sunbathing at certain times of the year. Instead, he told Ablat that he was sunbathing because he had just been engaged in bloodletting. This story is used by Fish (1981, p. 82) to prove that one is permitted to deceive a wicked person and thereby not provide him with a medical remedy.

Jewish law generally allows one to commit a sin if one's life is at stake. There are three serious transgressions, however, where a Jew is required to give up his life rather than violate Jewish law (*yehareg v'al ya'avor*): idolatry, illicit sexual relations with an *ervah* (e.g., adultery or incest between very close relatives), and murder (Babylonian Talmud, Sanhedrin 74a; Shulchan Aruch, Yoreh Deah, 157a). Jewish law does not obligate one to give up his or her life for other transgressions. Thus, if a Jew is told to desecrate the Sabbath or be killed, s/he should desecrate the Sabbath. (It should be noted that one may be obligated to become a martyr for a "lesser" transgression if the individual is told to violate the law publicly or if it is an epoch of forced conversion.) Lying is not, however, one of the three "serious" transgressions for which a Jew is obligated to become a martyr. There is however one possible exception to this rule. Is a Jew permitted to lie and say he is not Jewish in order not to be killed? Rabbi Abin mentions (Jerusalem Talmud, Avodah Zarah, 2:1) that a Jewish woman may save her life in a time of danger by saying that she is not Jewish. The Rosh, however, explains this passage differently and states that a Jew is not permitted to state that s/he is not Jewish,

even to save one's life since this is tantamount to denying one's religion. According to him, the above passage is talking about a Jewish woman dressing in a manner so that people believe that she is not Jewish in order to save herself. This would be permitted. The discussion by the commentaries over whether a Jew may lie and say he is not Jewish in order to save his life is very complex and beyond the scope of this paper.

Naaman the Aramean accepted monotheism after he was cured of his leprosy by the prophet Elisha (II Kings 5). He indicated, however, to Elisha that he would have to bow to the pagan deity, Rimon, when he accompanied his master to the House of Rimon since his master would lean on him while he prostrated himself. Elisha told him (II Kings 5: 19) to "go in peace" and, in effect, condoned the simulation of idol worshipping. Naaman was permitted to deceive his master rather than die for his beliefs since he had not converted to Judaism and thus only had the status of a Noachide who observes seven precepts (Babylonian Talmud, Sanhedrin 74b-75a).

According to the Talmud, Jacob distorted the truth when his brother Esau offered to accompany him (Genesis 33:12-16). Jacob, realizing that it might not be wise to travel with Esau, who might still harbor resentment over what happened regarding Isaac's blessing, told Esau (Genesis 33:14): "Let my lord go on ahead of his servant; while I will travel slowly at the pace of the work and at the pace of the children, until I come to my lord at Se'ir [Esau's land]." Of course, Jacob never went to Se'ir. The Midrash (Midrash Genesis Rabbah 78:14, cited by Rashi) notes that Jacob will one day go to Se'ir – in Messianic times. The Midrash is trying to show that Jacob did not actually lie.

The Talmud, however, derives an interesting principle from the above story that does permit lying in a potentially dangerous situation. The Talmud (Babylonian Talmud, Avodah Zarah 25b) states that one should always "broaden the journey" when speaking to idolaters [or anyone who could be a possible highwayman]. When asked about a destination, one should reply that he is traveling to a town that is actually well beyond his actual destination. The reason: If the idolater has plans to rob him along the way, he may wait until the Jewish traveler is near the end of the trip and by then the Jew will have already arrived at his destination. In fact, the Talmud notes that this stratagem saved the students of Rabbi Akiva from some armed robbers.

When Rabbi Eliezer was arrested by the authorities on suspicion of being a heretic, he saved himself by using a white lie involving some double talk (Babylonian Talmud, Avodah Zarah 16b-17a). The governor asked him: "How can a wise man such as you occupy himself with such nonsense?" Rabbi Eliezer replied: "I acknowledge the Judge as being right." The "Judge" Rabbi Eliezer referred to was God, not the judge who was interrogating him. The ruse worked and the governor said to him: "Because you have acknowledged me as being right, by *his* [the idol that the governor worshipped] mercy I am acquitting you."

There is another type of deception that is permitted where one's life may be in danger. Rabbi Shimon ben Pazi states (Babylonian Talmud, Sotah 41b) that "It is permitted to flatter wicked people in this world." He derives it from a verse in Isaiah (32:5) that refers to the Hereafter: "The vile person shall no longer be called generous, nor shall a deceitful person be said to be noble." Rabbi Shimon ben Lakish agrees but derives this ruling from a statement made by Jacob to Esau (Genesis 33:10): "for therefore I have seen your face, which is as though I had seen the face of a Divine being." This appears to contradict numerous negative statements about flattering evildoers such as "Every individual in whom there is flattery will fall into Hell," and "Whoever flatters the wicked [some texts have "his fellow human"] will eventually fall into his hand." (Babylonian Talmud, Sotah 41b). Tosafos explains this apparent contradiction by asserting that it is permitted to flatter the wicked in a dangerous, life-threatening situation. He provides proof for his view by citing a story involving Ulla who traveled with two people from Chozae to Israel (Babylonian Talmud, Nedarim 22a). One of his fellow travelers slaughtered the other and asked Ulla: "Did I do well?" Ulla replied in the affirmative and felt guilty but was later assured by Rabbi Yochanan in Israel that what he did was permitted since he said it to save his life.

The Talmud (Babylonian Talmud, Sanhedrin 29b) avers that "a person is accustomed not to make himself appear sated with wealth." This Talmudic principle is used to explain the reason that if an individual claims to owe another party money, we do not necessarily consider this as a true admission; this is why the "creditors" must furnish additional proof. Many people do not wish to arouse the envy of others so they pretend to be debtors.

Lying for the Sake Of Modesty or in Order Not to Appear Arrogant

There is an interesting story in the Talmud (Babylonian Talmud, Kethubos 77b) that supports the principle that one may utter a falsehood for the sake of modesty. When Rabbi Yehoshua ben Levi passed on to the next world, he was asked by Rabbi Shimon ben Yochai whether or not a rainbow ever appeared during his lifetime. A certain type of rainbow is a sign that the world actually deserves to be destroyed but is not because of God's promise to Noah after the Great Flood (see Genesis 11:12). Rabbi Yehoshua ben Levi responded in the affirmative. Rabbi Shimon ben Yochai replied: "Then you are not the son of Levi" since the merit of one true saint is sufficient to protect the entire world. The Talmud concludes, however, that the rainbow did not appear during Yehoshua ben Levi's lifetime. The reason he did not tell the truth was that "he did not want to boast about himself."

Another story in the Talmud (Babylonian Talmud, Taanis 23b) about Abba Chilkiyah also demonstrates that one may lie because of humility. The rabbis sent scholars to Abba Chikiyah during a drought to ask him to pray for rain. While the scholars were waiting for Abba to finish his meal, he surreptitiously went to the roof with his wife and prayed for rain. Clouds immediately appeared and it began to rain. He went back to the scholars and asked them why they had come, knowing very well the reason. Abba tried to convince the scholars that the rain came on its own accord, and not because of his (and his spouse's) prayer. The scholars, however, knew what had caused the rain to come.

Judaism also commands the converse of the above insofar as one is obligated to ensure that he does not benefit from others' misconception about his status or scholarship. The Talmud (Jerusalem Talmud, Maakot 2:6) states that if one is being honored by the public as a scholar who is proficient in two tractates but only knows one, he is obligated to disabuse the misconception and explicitly state "I am only knowledgeable in one tractate, and no more." Similarly, the Talmud earlier discusses the case of the scholar who is exiled to the city of refuge owing to his unintentional murder of another person. Should the people of the city wish to honor him, the scholar is duty-bound to proclaim that he is in town because he has taken a life.

Lying for the Sake of Decency

The following story/parable (Babylonian Talmud, Sanhedrin 97a) demonstrates the harm that may result from a lie for the sake of decency.

Rava said: At first I used to say that there is no truth in the world [i.e., that no person speaks the truth all the time]. Whereupon one of the Rabbis said to me, and Rabbi Tavus was his name, and some say Rabbi Tavyome was his name, that even if he would be given all the wealth in the world, he would not tell a lie. He related the following story: Once, I came to a certain town called Kushta [this name means truth in Aramaic] whose inhabitants would never tell a lie and no person ever died before his time.

He married a woman from among them and had two sons from her. One day his wife was sitting and washing her hair when a neighbor came and knocked on the door. Thinking to himself that it was not proper [to tell the neighbor that his wife was washing her hair], he said to the neighbor, "she is not here." His two sons died [as a punishment for his lying]. The people of the town came to him and asked, "What is the cause of this?" He related to them what had happened. They said to him: "We beg you to leave our town and do not incite death against us."

Rabbi Yaakov Emden explains why Rabbi Tavus was punished if one is permitted to lie for the sake of decency. In this case, Rabbi Tavus could have simply told the truth to the neighbor who would have understood and left; the white lie was totally unnecessary (Hagahos Yaakov Emden). Not all commentaries take the above story literally (e.g., Maharal).

Jacob's Deception of His Father

One of the more difficult cases of dishonesty to explain is Jacob's deception of his blind father, Isaac (Genesis 27). Was Jacob permitted to deceive his father and pretend to be Esau? Some commentaries take the approach that Jacob did not actually lie. When asked by his father who he was (Genesis 27:18), he replied: "I am Esau your

firstborn." Rashi and other commentators try to show that this was not really a falsehood. They say that Jacob responded as follows: "I am [the one who is bringing you the savory meats]; [whereas] Esau is your firstborn." Ibn Ezra does not accept this interpretation and points out that other prophets had to resort to deceptions. This difference of opinion also affects the explanation of a later verse (Genesis 27:35), when Isaac tells Esau: "your brother came with *mirmah* and took your blessing. Rashi interprets *mirmah* as wisdom; Ibn Ezra apparently translates it in the usual way, "deceit," because his comment on the word is that Jacob did not tell the truth. One important law that can be derived from the above is that if one does find himself or herself in a situation where they must lie, the correct way to do this is to use words that may have another meaning, vague statements, or through the use of half-truths (Chofetz Chaim, Hilchos Issurei Rechilus 1:8; Sefer Chassidim 642). This is somewhat similar to the "mental reservation" loophole discussed by Bok (1999, pp. 35-36). A mental reservation works as follows: "If you say something misleading to another and merely add a qualification to it in your mind so as to make it true, you cannot be responsible for the 'misinterpretation' made by the listener."

Nechama Liebowitz (1985, pp. 322-323) asserts that even the sages who take the side of Jacob "detect the workings of strict justice which is no respecter of persons, in what had befallen Jacob." She cites the following Midrash Tanchuma that describes what happened after Laban switched Leah for Rachel. Laban promised Jacob the hand of his beloved Rachel after seven years of labor.

All that night Leah pretended to be Rachel. When Jacob arose in the morning and saw that it was Leah, he said to her: "Daughter of the deceiver! Why did you deceive me? Leah said to him: And you, why did you deceive your father? When he said to you: "Are you my son Esau?" You replied (Genesis 27:19): "I am your son Esau." Yet you say to me, "why did I deceive you?" Did not your father say about you (Genesis 27:35): "Your brother came with guile."

It should be noted that the expression that Jacob uses when speaking to Laban after he switched Leah for Rachel is (Genesis 29:25): What is this that you have done to me? Was it not for Rachel that I served you? Why have you deceived [*rimitony*] me? The word used by Jacob is very similar to the word used to describe what Jacob had done to Esau. In fact, other commentators note that the words used in this passage "deceit," "younger," and "elder/firstborn" serve the purpose of reminding the reader of the similarity of the two situations, except that it is now Jacob who is being deceived by a substitution. Jacob is deceived several more times in his life. Laban switches his compensation several times (Genesis 31:7) and his children deceive him into believing that his beloved Joseph was dead. Whether Jacob was justified or not in deceiving his father, his entire life is turned upside down by deception.

Frimer (1973) uses a Midrash (Yalkut Shimoni, Genesis 29:12, Section 124; Midrash Genesis Rabbah 70:13) to make an interesting observation about dissembling. The Midrash, cited by Rashi, is on the following verse (Genesis 29:12): "And Jacob told Rachel that he was her father's brother [i.e., relative] and that he was Rebeccah's son; then she ran and told this to her father." There is an obvious redundancy in this verse, hence the Midrash: "If he comes to cheat, I am his brother in deceit; If he is an honorable man, then I am the son of Rebeccah [i.e., a man of integrity]." The Talmud (Babylonian Talmud, Baba Bathra 123a; Megilla 13b) has a slightly different explanation: Yaakov declares to Rachel that "I am his brother [match] in deceit." Rachel suspected that her father would try to deceive Jacob and try to make a substitution. The Talmud asks whether the righteous may indeed engage in deceit. The Talmud answers with the following verse (II Samuel 22:27): "with an honest person, act honestly; and with a corrupt person act perversely." Although this verse speaks of God, the Talmud is homiletically interpreting this verse to teach us that one may use guile when dealing with a cheat.

Frimer (1973) notes that Jacob tried his best to deal with Laban as honestly as possible (see Genesis 31:6-7). Moreover, Laban had a reputation for engaging in fraud. His reputation was so renowned that even his own daughter warned Jacob that her father was a cheat. Frimer therefore requires the following five conditions before allowing the honest person to "act perversely":

(1) The antagonist's record of general conduct is negative.

(2) There is adequate motivation and testimony to justify one's anticipated concern in the immediate and specific condition.

(3) The intended victim is acting only in self-defense and after the attack has been initiated.

(4) There appears to be no alternative to one's present course of action. Other options have been tried or are judged not to be viable.

(5) That which is at stake has tremendous seriousness to the intended victim involving a high investment of one's person or property.

Lying to Protect One's Property From Scoundrels

Frimer (1973) proves his position that deception is permitted when the above five conditions are met by citing the following case (Shulchan Aruch, Choshen Mishpat 335:5 based on Babylonian Talmud, Baba Metzia 75b):

When does this principle [that workers may not quit their job] apply? Where the loss is irreparable [davar ha'avud]. If the loss is irreparable, for example, if one hires laborers to remove his flax from the steeping water or hires a donkey-driver to bring flutists for the dead or for a bride, or something similar, then neither a laborer nor a contractor may quit his job unless there has been an emergency such as sickness or if he heard that there has been a death in the family.

The Shulchan Aruch states that if the worker, however, does attempt to quit when the loss is irreparable, and a replacement worker cannot be found, then the employer has a right to deceive the employee. This deception involves promising the laborer a much higher wage to continue working and then only paying the wage originally agreed upon after the work is completed. This is a case where the employer has much at stake (spoiled flax or a ruined wedding) and has no alternative (no replacement workers); therefore Jewish law allows one to be dishonest.

Fish (1981, pp.66) maintains that Rabbis Elyashiv, Fisher and Kanievsky were of the opinion that one may write "glass" on a package in order to ensure that it is handled properly, even if it does not contain glass. As proof, Rabbi

Kanievsky cites the Talmudic view (Babylonian Talmud, Yebamos 115b) that people would sometimes write "*terumah*" (consecrated to the priests) on a jar that did not contain unconsecrated produce as a means of protecting it, i.e., to ensure that people would not take it.

Daat Zekenim M'Baalei Tosafot (Genesis 25: 34) quotes Rabbi Yehuda HeChasid and states that one is permitted to deceive a wicked person who has a Torah scroll or another item used for a *mitzvah*. This principle is derived from Jacob who "tricked" Esau into selling his birthright to him (Genesis 25) for some lentils. According to the Daat Zekenim, Esau was abusing the birthright even before Jacob purchased it from him.

Habitual Lying

Dratch (1988) claims that even when prevaricating is permissible, habitual lying will still be forbidden. He uses the following Talmudic passage to support his position (Babylonian Talmud, Yebamos 63a):

Rav was constantly tormented by his wife. When he asked her to prepare him some lentils, she would prepare peas. When he asked for peas, she would prepare lentils. When Chiya, Rav's son, grew up, he would reverse his father's request. Once, Rav said to Chiya: "Your mother has improved." Rabbi Chiya replied: "It is I who reversed your requests to her." Rav remarked to Chiya: "This is what people say, 'Your own offspring teaches you reason.'" However, you should not continue to do so, for it says (Jeremiah 9:4): "They have taught their tongues to speak lies."

It is interesting to note that Rabbi Zera (Babylonian Talmud, Sukkot 46b) uses the same verse from Jeremiah (9:4) to make the point that one should not promise to a child that he will give him something and then not give it to him, because this will teach the child to lie.

Deceptions in Business

Lest one think that Jewish law is very flexible about lying for financial gain, the following is just a small sample of what one has to be concerned with. The Talmud has special rules about *geneivat da'at* (literally, theft of one's mind, thoughts, wisdom, or knowledge), i.e., fooling someone and thereby causing him or her to have a mistaken assumption, belief, and/or impression. The sages believed that there are seven types of thieves and, of these, the most egregious is the one who "steals the minds" of people (Tosefta Bava Kama 7:3). "Shmuel asserts (Babylonian Talmud, Chullin 94a-b): It is forbidden to steal the mind of anyone, even idolaters."

Geneivat da'at includes situations that result in someone getting undeserved goodwill (Babylonian Talmud, Chullin 94a), something considerably weaker than an outright lie. Thus, a person should not urge his friend to dine with him knowing that he will refuse. One should not offer gifts to another person knowing that the latter will not accept them. In a business setting, this would include misleading customers into thinking that the quality of the item they purchased is much better than it really is or making people believe they are getting a special deal when they are not. For additional information, see Friedman (2002).

Other kinds of deceptions that are prohibited include "deceiving the eye" by placing the better quality items in a bin on top in order to make it appear that the merchandise is of uniformly high quality throughout; soaking meat in water to make it appear fatter; and painting animals or utensils so that a buyer will think they are younger or newer (Babylonian Talmud, Baba Metzia 60a-b).

It is obvious that there are few situations where dissembling would be permitted in a business setting as a way of increasing one's profits. Rabbi Yonah (Shaarei Teshuvah 3: 178-186) describes nine types of liars and states explicitly that the businessperson who cheats others out of money is the worst of all. Another category of liar (third worst) is one whose prevarications cause someone to lose out on a future benefit or profit. For instance, making someone believe that a business deal is a bad idea when it really has excellent profit potential.

One situation that occurs quite frequently in business is where one party agrees to sell a product at a certain price. When the buyer shows up with the money, the seller changes his mind and asks for a higher price. Sometimes this occurs because market conditions have changed, i.e., prices have gone up or down. There is an argument in the Talmud (Babylonian Talmud, Baba Metzia 49a) as to whether a verbal commitment alone (i.e., no money has changed hands) to engage in a transaction obligates one from an ethical point of view to go through with the deal. Rav states that the individual who changes his mind is "not lacking in honesty." Rabbi Yochanan disagrees and says that the individual is "lacking in honesty." It is not clear whether this passage refers to a situation where market prices have changed.

The Shulchan Aruch (Choshen Mishpat 204:7) states that an individual who has made a verbal commitment, even if no money has changed hands, should stand by his word. People who retract after making a verbal commitment are "lacking in trustworthiness" and "the spirit of the sages is not pleased with him." There is a disagreement among the commentaries as to whether a person who changes his mind because the market price has changed is considered "lacking in trustworthiness." Several (e.g., Rosh, Tur) believe that a change in the market price is a legitimate reason for retracting and does not cause one to be considered as "lacking in honesty." The Remah (204:11) remarks that individuals who make verbal commitments to buy or sell —even if no *kinyan* (act of acquisition when title actually transfers) has taken place—should abide by their word; the "spirit of the sages is not pleased" with those who retract. If, however, the market price has changed, the individual who changes his mind about the deal is not considered "lacking in honesty."

The Aruch Hashulchan (Choshen Mishpat 204:8) asserts that if the market price has changed, and the seller therefore changes his mind about the selling price, he is not considered "lacking in honesty." It is, however, considered "the way of the pious" not to retract from a verbal agreement even if the market price has changed.

In Jewish law, title does not change hands until a *kinyan* (an act of acquisition) has been made by the acquirer. One example of a *kinyan* for a moveable object is *meshichah*, the act of pulling the object towards oneself. Suppose one party purchases an object from another party, money has changed hands, but there has been no *kinyan*. There is a public curse that may be proclaimed by the aggrieved party. The curse is as follows: "The One who punished the people of the generation of the Flood, the people of the generation of the Dispersion, the people of Sodom and Gomorrah, and the Egyptians in the sea, He will punish the person who does not stand by his word" (Babylonian Talmud, Baba Metzia 48a).

The Talmud lauds Rabbi Safra for his exemplary behavior in business and claims the verse (Psalms 15:2) "speaks truth in his heart" refers to individuals such as he. The Talmud (Maakot 24a, see commentary of Rashi) relates that one day, while Rabbi Safra was in the midst of prayer, a man offered to buy some merchandise from him. He made an offer, but Rabbi Safra was praying and could not respond. The prospective buyer mistakenly thought that Rabbi Safra was holding out for more, and kept increasing his bid. When Rabbi Safra finished his prayer, he told the buyer that he would sell the item at the original price because he had "agreed in his heart" to this price and his silence was misconstrued. Legally, of course, making up one's mind does not constitute a binding agreement but demonstrates an unusually high level of ethical behavior.

Rabbi Yehuda HeChasid (Sefer Chassidim, 311) states that merchants are prohibited from misleading customers by falsely claiming that another party wishes to pay so much for the item or by stating how much that they paid for the merchandise when it is not true. Regarding these type of deceptions the verse (Zephaniah 3:13) avers: "The remnant of Israel shall do no wrong, and not speak falsehood, and a deceitful tongue shall not be found in their mouths."

Rabbi Yehuda HeChasid (Sefer Chassidim, 395) tells a story of a businessman who wanted to know how to gain the World-to-Come (i.e., Paradise) if he had no time for studying Torah, except for the Sabbath. He was told by a rabbi to conduct his business as follows: giving something extra to the buyer when weighing out the merchandise, being honest in business with Jew and Gentile, doing business with a friendly disposition, not losing one's temper, not being overly trusting (by lending money without witnesses one may tempt others to steal), and paying one's debts on time. "If you heed the above principles," the rabbi stated, "then I wish that my share in the World-to-Come would be equivalent to yours."

Fish (1981, pp. 79-80) discusses the question as to whether one may lie in order to get back money that was stolen from him. He uses the following story from the Talmud (Babylonian Talmud, Yuma 83b) to prove that it is permissible. Before the Sabbath, Rabbi Yehuda and Rabbi Yosi asked their host, Kidor, to hold their money for safekeeping. When the Sabbath ended, they asked Kidor to return their money; he denied ever having been given anything. Subsequently, they saw him outside with lentils on his moustache. They surmised that he had eaten lentils. They went to his house and told his wife that her husband requested that she return their money and as a sign that they were telling the truth, he told them to tell her that he had eaten lentils for his meal.

Other Situations Involving Lying

The Talmud (Babylonian Talmud, Kallah Rabbathi, 2) relates that Rabbi Tarfon was wealthy but did not give as much to charity as he was capable. Rabbi Akiva offered to purchase some cities for him and he was given four thousand gold *dinarim*. Rabbi Akiva took the money and distributed it to poor people. When Rabbi Tarfon asked where the cities were, Rabbi Akiva took him to the house of study and brought a schoolchild who read the verse from Psalms (112:9) "he [the righteous person] distributed widely to the impoverished." Some use this story to prove that deception may be permitted in some situations involving charity collection to help the impoverished (Fish, pp. 54-55).

Fish (1981. p. 197) cites several sources that indicate that one should lie to an individual who is very ill when the truth could demoralize the person and possibly hasten his death. Thus, one should not tell a sick person that his friend has died, if he asks how the person is doing, especially if the individual passed away from the same illness.

The Talmud (Babylonian Talmud, Shabbos 116a-b) relates a story of how Imma Shalom and her brother Rabbi Gamliel pretended to be involved in a dispute in order to expose a heretical judge. The judge had an undeserved reputation for honesty and they went to him to settle their "dispute" over the division of their deceased father's estate. The judge ended up taking bribes from both of them. Apparently, they felt that the situation called for lying, in order to expose the corrupt judge.

In an example of the sages' concern for potentially conveying an appearance of falsehood, the Talmud (Babylonian Talmud Sanhedrin 30a) rules that when a judicial verdict is handed down via majority (not unanimously), the decision is proclaimed "through the words of the Court, so and so was found not liable." This is the opinion of Rabbi Elazar and is the *halacha*. Rabbi Yochanan's opinion was that the verdict is written simply as "not liable" since Rabbi Yochanan was concerned with the problem of gossip mongering (prohibited by the Torah – see Leviticus 19:16). Revealing how the individual judges voted is tantamount to gossip mongering. After all, little good can come from the losing party knowing which judges voted against him. Resh Lakish disagrees with Rabbi Yochanan and says the wording must indicate which judge voted to acquit and which judge found the defendant liable; otherwise, the verdict will appear to be untrue. The view of Rabbi Elazar protects the truth and, at the same time, does not violate the prohibition against gossip mongering.

There is a problematic story in the Talmud (Babylonian Talmud, Berachos 43b) that suggests that Rabbi Pappa fabricated a legal statement in order to avoid embarrassment. The Talmud first discusses the dispute between the Schools of Shammai and Hillel as to which blessing is made first when one is given oil and myrtle at the end of a meal (fragrant oil was used to clean off the food odors and the myrtle was smelled for its pleasant scent). The School of Shammai states that the blessing is first made over the oil and then over the myrtle; the School of Hillel disagrees and says that the benediction over the myrtle is made first. Rabbi Gamliel said that he would "decide" the issue and favors the opinion of the School of Shammai (since oil has two uses whereas the myrtle only has one). Rabbi Yochanan (in a later generation) asserted: "the law is in accordance with the decider."

Rabbi Pappa was at the house of Rabbi Huna ben Ika and they brought oil and myrtle before him and he made the blessing on the myrtle before the oil. Rabbi Huna was surprised and asked: "Does not the master hold that "the law was in accordance with the decider." The Talmud then states that Rabbi Pappa was ashamed of having done something wrong so he told a falsehood and claimed that Rava had stated that the law is agreement with the School of Hillel, a statement that Rava had never made. This story presents many difficulties. However, according to Tosafos and Rif there is an error in the text and they delete the phrase that says Rabbi Pappa made up the statement of Rava. Those who delete the phrase obviously believe that lying about a legal matter in order to avoid embarrassment is not allowed. This is clearly true. An alternative explanation, however, of the above story is that Rabbi Pappa did not agree with the view of Rabbi Yochanan and rather than stating that he did not agree and that the law is in accordance with the School of Hillel, he attributed the statement to his teacher, Rava (see Rama MiPano). According to this view, if one is absolutely sure of a law, one, because of modesty, may attribute it to someone else.

Conclusion

This paper demonstrates that Jewish law does not take an absolutist approach to prevaricating and, indeed, will obligate the individual to lie in various circumstances, for instance, lying to save a life or to bring peace. This, by no means, makes light of the seriousness of lying. The Talmud is replete with statements that stress the importance of truth-telling and remarks that "the seal of God is *emeth* [truth]" (Babylonian Talmud, Shabbat 55a); "God hates one who speaks one thing with his mouth and another thing in his heart" (Babylonian Talmud, Pesachim 113b); "Whoever breaks his word is regarded as though he has worshiped idols" (Babylonian Talmud, Sanhedrin 92a); and "liars will not receive the Divine Presence (Babylonian Talmud, Sotah 42a)." The extreme importance of honesty is appropriately summed up by the Talmudic belief that the first question a person is asked in the hereafter at the final judgment is (Babylonian Talmud, Shabbat 31a): "Have you been honest in your dealings?" Despite all this, the Talmud recognizes that there are situations where one may be untruthful.

References

Aquinas, Thomas (1947), *The Summa Theologica*, Benziger Bros. Edition, Translated by Fathers of the English Dominican Province, <http://www.ccel.org/a/aquinas/summa/home. html>, (February 2003).

Augustine (2002), *De Mendacio, New Advent*, <http://www. newadvent.org/fathers/1312.htm>, (February 2003).

Bok, Sisella (1999), *Lying: Moral Choice in Public and Private Life*, New York: Vintage Books.

Catholic Encyclopedia (2002), "Lying," *New Advent*, <http:// www.newadvent.org/cathen/09469a.htm> (February 2003).

Dratch, Mark (1988), "Nothing but the Truth," *Judaism,* Vol. 37 (2), Spring. Also on the Web at: <http://www.agudathsholom. org/wrmd-nothingbutthetruth.htm>.

Fish, Yaakov (1981), *Titen Emes L'Yaakov*, Jerusalem: Self-Published.

Friedman, Hershey (2002), "Geneivat Da'at: The Prohibition Against Deception in Today's World," *Jewish Law*, <http://www. jlaw.com/Articles/geneivatdaat.html>, (March 2003).

Frimer, Norman (1973), "A Midrash on Morality or When is a Lie Permissible," *Tradition,* Vol. 13, Spring-Summer, pp. 23-34.

Geary, James (2000), "Deceitful Minds: The Awful Truth About Lying," *Time Europe,* Vol. 155 (10), 56-61.

Grotius, Hugo (1925), *On the Law of War and Peace*, translated by F. Kelsey, Indianapolis: Bobbs-Merrill.

Liebowitz, Nechama (1985), Studies in Shemot, translated by Aryeh Newman, Jerusalem: World Zionist Organization.

Nyberg, David (1993), *The Varnished Truth: Truth Telling & Deceiving in Ordinary Life*, Chicago: University of Chicago Press.

Sidgwick, Henry (1966), *The Methods of Ethics*, New York: Dover Publications [Originally published in 1907].

Walsh, John (2001), "So, How Many Lies Have You Told Today?" *The Independent--London,* January 17.

Yabrov, Nochum (2000), *Niv Sefasayim*, Jerusalem: Self-Published.

http://www.jlaw.com/Articles/hf_LyingPermissible.html

Lesson 6
Penny for Your Thoughts
Fair Use and Copyright in Talmudic Law

Introduction

n 1774, William Enfield made the following argument in support of the idea of copyright:

"In this various world different men are born to different fortunes: one inherits a portion of land; he cultivates it with care, it produces him corn and fruits and wool: another possesses a fruitful mind, teeming with ideas of every kind; he bestows his labor in cultivating that; the produce is reason, sentiment, philosophy. It seems but equitable, that a fair exchange should be made of these goods; and that one man should live by the labor of his brain, as well as another by the sweat of his brow."

Observation on Literary Property (London, 1774), 21-22.

Intuitively, it seems correct that people should be able to reap the profit of their own ideas.

Is there a basis in the Talmud for this idea as well?

That is the subject of this lesson.

Introduction to
the Question of Copyright

Text 1

To promote the Progress of Science and useful Arts, by securing for limited Times to Authors and Inventors the exclusive Right to their respective Writings and Discoveries;

UNITED STATES CONSTITUTION, ARTICLE I, SECTION 8

Origins of Copyright Law
Case Study

Dear Rabbi Natansohn,

Mr. Abraham Goldberg, a publisher of Hebrew books in Levov, is suing Mr. Hirsh Balaban who wishes to print a set of *Shulchan Aruch* [Code of Jewish Law by Rabbi Yosef Karo] with the commentary *Pri To'ar*. Goldberg claims that he bought the rights to this commentary from the author himself. Does Goldberg have any claim against Balaban?

Sincerely,

Shmuel Valdberg, Chief Rabbi of Zalkova

Rabbi Yosef Shaul Natansohn, Responsa Sho'el U'Meishiv, vol. 1, no. 44

Rabbi Yosef Shaul Natansohn (1808–1875) was a leading rabbinical authority of his day. In 1857 he was elected Rabbi of Lemberg, where he officiated for eighteen years. His rulings are still widely cited.

Copyright as a Societal Convention

Text 2 📖

אמר שמואל: דינא דמלכותא דינא

Shmuel said: The law of the land must be obeyed by Torah Law.

TALMUD, GITTIN 10B

Text 3 📖

רשאין החמרין להתנות שכל מי שיאבד לו חמורו יעמיד לו חמור אחר
בכוסיא: אין מעמידין; שלא בכוסיא: מעמידין לו

The donkey-drivers are entitled to stipulate that one who loses his donkey should be provided with another donkey. [If, however, this was caused] by negligence, they would not have to provide him with another donkey; where this was done without any negligence [on his part], he is provided with another donkey.

TALMUD, BAVA KAMA 116A

Text 4 📖

וכן מנהג התגרים שנוהגים כן תמיד
אף על פי שלא הסכימו בכך ולא התנו כן . . .
מן הסתם על מי שנושא ונותן סתם על הדבר הנוהג הוא עושה
וכאלו התנו ביניהן בפירוש או שתקנו להם בית דין

If merchants consistently conduct themselves according to a custom, even if they did not formally agree to this custom nor did they verbally stipulate it . . . we may presume that anyone engaging in trade is doing so on account of this custom and the custom is, therefore, binding on all merchants, as if it were expressly stipulated between the merchants or regulated by the *Beit Din* [courts].

<small>RABBI SHLOMO BEN ADERET, TESHUVOT HARASHBA, VOL. 2, NO. 268</small>

Rabbi Shlomo ben Aderet (Rashba) (1235–1310) was a halachist and Talmudist. He was a successful banker in Barcelona, and leader of Spanish Jewry of his time. His teachers were the Ramban and Rabbeinu Yonah.

Origins of Copyright in the Talmud

Hasagat Gevul: Unfair Encroachment

Text 5

עושה אדם חנות בצד חנותו של חבירו

ומרחץ בצד מרחצו של חבירו

ואינו יכול למחות בידו

מפני שיכול לומר לו: אתה עושה בתוך שלך ואני עושה בתוך שלי

אמר רב הונא בריה דרב יהושע:

פשיטא לי בר מתא אבר מתא אחריתי מצי מעכב

A person may open a rival store next to the store of his fellow, and the established operator cannot prevent him from doing so, because the rival can say to the established operator,

"You do as you wish inside your property, and I do as I wish in my property . . . ."

Rav Huna son of Rav Yehoshua said, "It is obvious to me that a resident of one town who plies a certain trade can prevent a resident of another town from plying that trade anywhere in his town."

TALMUD, BAVA BATRA 21B

Copyright as Ownership of an Idea

Text 6

"אל תגזל דל כי דל הוא" אמר רבי שמעון בן יוחאי . . .
כל שאינו אומר דבר בשם אומרו עובר בלאו
שנאמר "אל תגזל דל כי דל הוא"

"Don't steal from a poor man, for he is poor (Mishlei/Proverbs 22:22)." Rabbi Shimon bar Yochai . . . said, "Someone who does not credit the source of an original statement when repeating it to others is in violation of the verse, 'Don't steal from a poor man.'"

YALKUT SHIMONI, PROVERBS 22:22

Text 7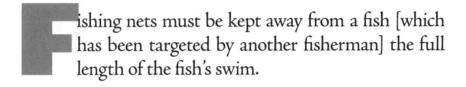

מרחיקים מצודת הדג מן הדג כמלא ריצת הדג

Fishing nets must be kept away from a fish [which has been targeted by another fisherman] the full length of the fish's swim.

Talmud, Bava Batra 21b

Text 8

I was asked by someone from Livorno the following question:

Reuben authored a commentary on the Talmud and wished to have it published together with the text of the Talmud. He negotiated a fee with Simon, a publisher, to have the text of the Talmud printed along with the classic commentaries of Rashi and Tosafot on each side and the author's commentary on the bottom of each page.

Ordinarily, after the printing of a book is completed, printers dismantle the arrangement of the letters on the plate so that the letters will be available for other printing endeavors. However, in this case, Simon (the publisher), who owned many sets of letters for other printing projects, decided to leave the arrangement of the letters designed for Reuben's publication on the plate. Simon intended to take advantage of the long hours and hard work that was invested in creating these plates, in order to be able to publish in the future a regular edition of the Talmud with the classical commentaries, without Reuben's commentary.

Reuben claims that since he paid for the work of arranging the letters of the Talmudic texts, Simon has no right to benefit from this arrangement in the future without granting Simon a share in the profits of the second printing of the Talmud. On the other hand, Simon argues that since the actual physical letters belong to him, he has the right to use them as he pleases. Reuben has no right to demand that he destroy the arrangement on the plates.

Rabbi Yechezkel Landau
She'eilot UTeshuvot Noda Be'Yehudah, vol. 2, Choshen Mishpat, no. 24

Rabbi Yechezkel Landau (1713–1779) Chief Rabbi of Prague and head of the Yeshiva there, was an influential authority in Halachah. He is best known for the work *Noda Be'Yehudah*, one of the principal sources of Jewish law of his age.

Text 9

אמר ליה רב חסדא לרמי בר חמא: . . . הדר בחצר חבירו שלא מדעתו
צריך להעלות לו שכר או אין צריך?
. . . בחצר דלא קיימא לאגרא וגברא דעביד למיגר, מאי?
מצי אמר ליה מאי חסרתיך או דלמא מצי אמר הא איתהנית?
. . . אמר ליה רבה בר רב הונא: הכי אמר אבא מרי משמיה דרב:
אינו צריך להעלות לו שכר

Rav Chisda said to Rami bar Chamah: If one lives in the yard of his fellow without the latter's knowledge, does he have to pay him rent or not?

. . . . The question is in regard to a yard that is not for rent but [the squatter] is a person who usually rents. What is the law?

Can the squatter say to the owner, "What loss have I caused you?"

Or perhaps the owner can say to him, "Why, you have benefited!" [the squatter would have had to rent different quarters . . . .]

[The Talmud concludes:] Rabah the son of Rav Huna said, "Thus did my father, my master say in the name of Rav: 'He does not have to pay him rent.'"

TALMUD, BAVA KAMA 20A-21B

Text 10

תא שמע: הבית והעלייה של שנים שנפלו
אמר בעל העלייה לבעל הבית לבנות והוא אינו רוצה
הרי בעל העלייה בונה בית ויושב בה עד שיתן לו יציאותיו
רבי יהודה אומר: אף זה הדר בחצר חבירו שלא מדעתו . . .
צריך להעלות לו שכר
שמע מינה: זה נהנה וזה לא חסרחייב
שאני התם משום שחרוריתא דאשייתא

Come, learn [a proof that a squatter is obligated to pay] from the following Mishnah: [If a ground story and upper story owned by two different people collapsed, and the owner of the upper story told the owner of the ground story to rebuild the ground story so that he would be able to rebuild his upper story on top of it, but the owner of the ground story does not want to rebuild, then the owner of the upper story may rebuild the ground story on his own and live in it until the owner of the ground story pays him his expenses (i.e., the amount he expended in having the ground story rebuilt)] . . . . Rabbi Yehudah says:

The owner of the upper story who lives on the premises of his fellow without the latter's knowledge, must pay him rent. Learn from this that where this one benefits and this one does not lose, the one who benefits is obligated to pay.

[The Talmud rejects this proof:] It is different there, because of the blackening of the walls.

TALMUD, BAVA KAMA 21A

Text 11

He [the printer] has caused a great loss [to the author], for if the printer had not published these [second] books, there would have been a great demand for Reuben's [the author's] work [which included the Talmudic text] . . . . Now, that Simon [the printer] has printed [his volumes], these volumes which are cheap and in great supply will reduce the demand for Reuben's work. Since the printer has caused the author a financial loss, we obligate him to pay all that he benefited from the author's share in the typeset arrangement.

SHE'EILOT UTESHUVOT NODA BE'YEHUDAH, OP. CIT., VOL. 2, CHOSHEN MISHPAT, NO. 24

The Moral and the Mystical

Text 12

רב גידל הוה מהפיך בההיא ארעא, אזל רבי אבא זבנה

אזל רב גידל קבליה לרבי זירא

אזל רבי זירא וקבליה לרב יצחק נפחא

אמר ליה: המתן עד שיעלה אצלנו לרגל

כי סליק אשכחיה אמר ליה: עני מהפך בחררה ובא אחר ונטלה הימנו, מאי?

אמר ליה: נקרא רשע

ואלא מר מאי טעמא עבד הכי? אמר ליה: לא הוה ידענא

השתא נמי ניתבה ניהליה מר

אמר ליה: זבוני לא מזבינא לה, דארעא קמייתא היא ולא מסמנא מילתא

אי בעי במתנה נישקליה

רב גידל לא נחית לה, דכתיב: "ושונא מתנות יחיה"

רבי אבא לא נחית לה משום דהפיך בה רב גידל

לא מר נחית לה ולא מר נחית לה, ומיתקריא ארעא דרבנן

Rav Gidel was attempting to purchase a plot of land. Rav Abba pre-empted him and purchased the plot. Rav Gidel mentioned this incident to Rabbi Zeira who in turn related the incident to Rav Yitzchak Nafcha. Rav Yitzchak Nafcha told him to wait and that he would discuss the matter with Rav Abba when the latter would come and visit him before Yom Tov.

When Rav Abba arrived, Rav Yitzchak asked him, "When a poor person is attempting to acquire a loaf of bread, and another comes and takes it away from him, how does one view such a person?" [He is attempting to acquire an abandoned loaf, or to convince its owner to donate it to him—Rashi]

Rav Abba replied: "He is called a *rasha* [an immoral person]." [Since he is intruding on someone else's livelihood—Rashi]

Rav Yitzchak asked: "In that case why did you engage in such an activity [in regard to the plot of land Rav Gidel was trying to purchase]?"

He replied, "I did not know [that Rav Gidel was trying to purchase it]!"

Rav Yitzchak asked: "Perhaps now you will sell it to Rav Gidel?"

Rav Abba replied: "I do not wish to sell it, since it is a bad sign to sell the first piece of property one acquires. However, I am prepared to give it as a gift to Rav Gidel."

Rav Gidel said: "I do not want gifts, since the verse states, 'One who despises handouts will live long (Mishlei 15:27).'" But Rav Abba did not wish to own the land either, because Rav Gidel had tried to acquire it. In the end, neither of them claimed ownership of the field; rather it was made available for the use of all the rabbis and it came to be called "the land of the rabbis."

TALMUD, KIDUSHIN 59A

Text 13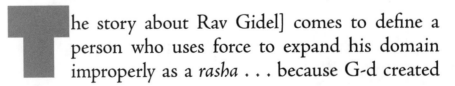

The story about Rav Gidel] comes to define a person who uses force to expand his domain improperly as a *rasha* . . . because G-d created man and designated a livelihood for each and every person . . . . Just as two hairs do not grow out of the same pore (Talmud, Bava Batra 16a), . . . G-d gives each person his individual source of nourishment . . . so that he need not encroach upon that which is designated for his friend. If he does interfere with another's livelihood, this is regarded as theft . . . and worse than theft, since it meddles with the portion that G-d allotted for each individual.

R. Yehudah Loew (Maharal of Prague)
Netivot Olam, Netiv HaTzedakah, ch. 3

Rabbi Yehudah Loew of Prague (1525–1609), "The *Maharal*," thinker and mystic. Author of *Gevurat HaShem*. Thousands visit his resting place in the old Jewish cemetery of Prague.

Text 14

Our Sages declared that "the Torah has sympathy for our possessions (Rosh HaShanah 27a)." The Ba'al Shem Tov explains: Our possessions are valuable to the Almighty because there are sparks of holiness imbedded in them and it is a person's duty to extract them and elevate them to holiness . . . .

The order in which these sparks of holiness are extracted and their relevance to our souls is as follows: just as it is predetermined for each spark who will extract it, so too is it determined which sparks each soul must extract, for those sparks are pertinent to that particular soul. This is the meaning of what our Sages state, "One person cannot touch what is set aside for his friend (Yoma 33b)," for it is impossible to earn a living from that which belongs to another.

Rabbi Menachem Mendel Schneerson (1902–1994), "the Lubavitcher Rebbe," also known simply as "the Rebbe." Born in southern Ukraine. Rabbi Schneerson escaped from the Nazis, arriving in the US in June 1941. The Rebbe, the towering Jewish leader of the twentieth century, inspired and guided the revival of traditional Judaism after the European devastation, and often emphasized that the performance of just one additional good deed could usher in the era of Mashiach.

This is true in the material world because it is true in the spiritual world (spiritual "profits" are the sparks of holiness imbedded in material objects)—and each soul has its duty to extract certain sparks that are pertinent to that soul by virtue of its nature . . . . Furthermore, the extraction and elevation of those sparks is related to the essence of a person's soul.

RABBI MENACHEM MENDEL SCHNEERSON (THE LUBAVITCHER REBBE)
LIKUTEI SICHOT, VOL. 3, P. 824-5

Key Points

1. Copyright has only become common in secular courts since the advent of the printing press made it easy to reproduce written works in large quantities for profit. So any attempt to find support for the notion of copyright in Jewish law must come by way of analogy to some comparable law.

2. Torah requires us to respect the law of the land, as well as the assumed ethical standards of a given profession.

3. The prohibition underlying Torah's legal regulation of unfair competition is called *hasagat gevul,* literally, "moving another's boundary." The Talmud applies this concept to encroaching on another's livelihood.

4. One who benefits from the property of another while causing the owner a loss is liable to the owner. Rabbi Landau believes this principle can apply even to the owner of an intangible creation, such as the author who commissions a particular design of print.

5. On the spiritual plane, the mystics explain that each person is given his/her designated source of sustenance, and need not encroach on another's. Every individual is responsible for the "sparks" of divine energy within his own domain, and thus, to preempt another's acquisition of property—which is connected to his particular spiritual destiny—is a transgression of the true spiritual order.

Additional Readings

Hasagat Gevul: Economic Competition in Jewish Law

by **Rabbi Chaim Jachter**[*]

Hasagat gevul (literally "infringement of boundary") is often used to refer to unfair business competition.[1] In the past few years, many accusations of *hasagat gevul* have been brought before *batei din*. These cases often arouse much controversy, especially since the Halachah is sometimes at odds with American society's tendency to favor unrestricted competition.

Aggadic Background

Before examining the halachic texts that address this issue, there are two relevant aggadic passages from the Gemara. While aggadic passages are usually not halachically binding,[2] they do set a tone that influences halachic decisions. In *Yevamot* (78b), the Gemara draws an equation between eliminating an individual's ability to earn a livelihood and murder. In *Makkot* (24a), the Gemara records that King David outlined eleven fundamental principles of halachic life, among them that one should not compete with another person's business. These passages give moral weight to those who generally favor restricting business competition.

The Gemara

The primary halachic discussion of business competition appears in *Bava Batra* (21b). The Gemara records that one may not set up a fishing net too close to another person's fishing net and thus catch all the fish that would have gone into the original net. Because the fish would have otherwise gravitated automatically to the original net, they are viewed as if they have already reached its owner's possession.[3] However, *Amoraim* dispute a less flagrant form of competition, in which one person is operating a mill in a *mavuy* (alley),[4] and another wishes to open a similar establishment there. Does the first person have the right to prevent his competitor from opening in the same *mavuy*?

Rav Huna asserts that the owner of the first mill may prevent the newcomer from setting up shop, as the new-comer will interfere with the first inhabitant's livelihood. Rav Huna the son of Rav Yehoshua, on the other hand, argues that this is permitted. Rashi (s.v. *Shani Dagim*) explains that the competitor may claim, "Whoever will come to me will come to me, and whoever will come to you will come to you." The Gemara indicates that the latter position fits with the majority opinion in a similar debate from the time of the *Tannaim* (see *Tosafot, Bava Batra* 21b s.v. *Peshita*). The Gemara thus seems to permit starting a competitive business, if its owner does not aim to inflict direct damage on his opposition.

The Halachah normally follows the majority opinion,[5] and the Halachah generally follows the later *Amora*,[6] so virtually all *Rishonim*[7] follow Rav Huna the son of Rav Yehoshua's view, as do the *Shulchan Aruch* (*Choshen Mishpat* 156:5) and most of its commentaries (see *Aruch Hashulchan, Choshen Mishpat* 156:6-7). The Rif, Rambam, and *Shulchan Aruch* do not even mention the Gemara's restriction regarding the fishing nets, so perhaps they understood that the Gemara eventually rejected that law. In fact, the Meiri (*Bava Batra* 21b) explicitly rejects the restriction on setting new fishing nets near old ones. It would thus seem that the Halachah sanctions nearly unrestricted free enterprise.

Nonetheless, Rav Huna the son of Rav Yehoshua adds that such competition is only permitted when the new competitor comes from the same *mavuy*, for he is just as entitled as the first businessman to earn a livelihood in that area. The new competitor can claim, "You do work on your home turf, and [so too] I do work on my home turf." However, one who comes from a different city and challenges the established local business is unfairly encroaching. Rav Huna the son of Rav Yehoshua inquires whether one who comes from a different *mavuy* but resides in the same city is considered sufficiently local to be granted the right to compete. Due to the fact that the Gemara never reaches a conclusion regarding such a person (*teiku*), the *Rishonim* rule that there is insufficient basis for preventing a resident of another *mavuy* in the same city from opening a competing business.[8] The *Shulchan Aruch* (*Choshen Mishpat* 156:5) rules accordingly.

The Gemara adds that even an outsider is permitted to compete if he pays taxes to the local authority. The *Tur* (*ibid.*) writes that an outsider who pays taxes is permitted to compete "like the residents of the city," and the *Shulchan Aruch* (*ibid.*) accepts this presentation. However, *Tosafot* (*Bava Batra* 21b s.v. *Ve'i*) assert that, even if the outside resident pays taxes to the local authority, he may only open a business in a **different** *mavuy* in that city. The Rama rules like *Tosafot*.[9]

The Aviasaf's Interpretation

As mentioned above, Rav Huna the son of Rav Yehoshua appears to permit most competition, and, according to the Meiri (and possibly Rambam, Rif, and *Shulchan Aruch*), he does not even prohibit placing one's fishing net right in front of someone else's net. Even if one assumes that Rav Huna the son of Rav Yehoshua does prohibit placing the fishing net in such a manner, it is still not clear what level of competition he means to prohibit. The case of the fishing nets might be a uniquely extreme case, as the fish were sure to go into the original net. Alternatively, that case might come to prohibit any new store that will undoubtedly cripple the original store's income, even if the new entrepreneur does not directly block the incumbent's merchandise. Consequently, there has been a dispute since the time of the *Rishonim* regarding where to draw the line between legitimate economic competition and unfair damage to someone else's livelihood.

The *Aviasaf* (cited by the Mordechai, *Bava Batra* 516, and *Hag'hot Maimoniot, Hil. Shecheinim* 6:8) defines unfair competition in a most broad manner. He forbids opening a store at the entrance to a *mavuy satum* (a dead-end alley) if a similar establishment is already located farther within the *mavuy satum*. Such competition is unfair, for it will definitely ruin the original shopkeeper's business. Potential customers will see the new store upon entering the *mavuy satum* without ever noticing the other establishment farther in. Rav Yosef Karo (*Beit Yosef, Choshen Mishpat* 156 s.v. *Vekatav Hamordechai*) claims that the *Aviasaf* is following Rav Huna's opinion in the Gemara (prohibiting opening a new mill where one already exists). As mentioned above, most *Rishonim* rule against Rav Huna (in favor of Rav Huna the son of Rav Yehoshua). Rav Karo thus ignores the *Aviasaf*'s view in his *Shulchan Aruch* (C.M. 156:5) and rules that all local competitors are unrestricted in their ability to open rival businesses.

The Rama (*Darchei Moshe* 156:4), however, explains that, according to the *Aviasaf*, even the lenient[10] Rav Huna the son of Rav Yehoshua prohibits opening a new business at the start of a *mavuy satum*. The reason for this is that the new business will surely cripple the business inside the *mavuy*. Not surprisingly, therefore, the Rama takes a stricter stance than the *Shulchan Aruch*, for he understands that the *Aviasaf*'s ruling fits into the accepted position in the Gemara. In a responsum (10), the Rama adjudicates a famous sixteenth-century dispute between two Italian publishers who both printed editions of the Rambam's *Mishneh Torah*. The one who published it first objected to the existence of a rival edition of the *Mishneh Torah*. The Rama rules against the second publisher, reasoning (based on the *Aviasaf*'s ruling) that all *Amoraim* forbid opening a store if it will clearly ruin the original entrepreneur's business. The Rama thus concludes that the second publisher should not be patronized, as he was unfairly ruining the original publisher's livelihood.

Other Limitations on Competition

Even if one does not accept the *Aviasaf*'s ruling, it is still possible to apply some limits to free enterprise. For example, the *Mas'at Binyamin* (27, quoted by *Pitchei Teshuvah, Choshen Mishpat* 156:3) addresses a town that was permitted to have only one store of a particular type. One such store already existed, and someone wanted to start an identical one. The *Mas'at Binyamin* writes that even the lenient Rav Huna the son of Rav Yehoshua forbids the new competitor from opening. Since there was not even a theoretical chance of both stores surviving, the new storeowner was assuredly damaging the incumbent (*bari hezeika*). The *Pitchei Teshuvah* points out that nowhere in his responsum does the *Mas'at Binyamin* cite the *Aviasaf*'s ruling as a precedent. Perhaps the *Mas'at Binyamin* would permit opening a store at the entrance to a *mavuy satum*. Regarding a *mavuy satum*, at least some chance exists that people will decide to walk into the *mavuy* and buy from the original merchant, even if this is unlikely. In this town, by contrast, the law made it completely impossible for two stores of the same type to coexist.

The Rashba (*Teshuvot* 3:83) also limits free enterprise. He extrapolates from the Gemara's case of the fishing nets that, while one may open a rival business, he may not actively pursue people who are known to be regular customers of the first proprietor. Just as one who places his net in front of the first net swipes fish that were heading straight toward it, this type of advertising steals customers who would have undoubtedly bought from the original proprietor.

Responsa of Acharonim

The *Chatam Sofer* (*Choshen Mishpat* 61 and 118, cited by *Pitchei Teshuvah* 156:3) understands that even Rav Huna the son of Rav Yehoshua permits competition when the new store will only **decrease** the profits of the original proprietor. However, competition that will **eliminate** the original proprietor's ability to earn a livelihood is forbidden. The *Chatam Sofer* quotes the *Aviasaf* as a precedent and asserts that Rashi agrees with the *Aviasaf*. Rashi (mentioned above) explains that the lenient view in the Gemara permits competition because "whoever will come to me will come to me, and whoever will come to you will come to you." Surely, argues the *Chatam Sofer*, Rashi would agree that if the new competitor's presence made it nearly impossible for consumers to go to his rival's store, this claim is untenable. Everyone would forbid opening the new store in such a case. The *Chatam Sofer* thus concludes that none of the *Amoraim* ever sanctioned destroying someone else's livelihood completely.

The *Chatam Sofer* (*Choshen Mishpat* 79) adds that a community may administer lashes to one who competes unfairly. He bases this on the aforementioned responsa of the Rama (who appears to forbid non-Jews, too, from competing unfairly) and *Mas'at Binyamin*, both of which view unfair competition as a heinous offense. It is worth noting that the *Chatam Sofer* explicitly prohibits unfair competition even when the original merchant knows another trade or can support himself with other money.

Not all *Acharonim* subscribe to the *Chatam Sofer*'s limitations on competition. For example, the *Chatam Sofer* notes that the *Chavot Ya'ir* (*Teshuvot* 42) actually derives the reverse from the aggadic passage (cited above from *Makkot* 24a) in which King David praises one who does not enter his fellow's trade. The *Chavot Ya'ir* reasons that David considers this trait a sign of **piety** precisely because it is **technically permitted** (as long as one is a local resident). David commends one who refrains from

competing with his friend for going **beyond** the letter of the law.[11] The *Pitchei Teshuvah* also cites the *Beit Efrayim* (*Choshen Mishpat* 26-27), who writes that common practice in his community was apparently not to follow the *Aviasaf*'s view. His community permitted entrepreneurs to open new hotels at the city gate, despite the fact that all who entered the city saw the new hotels before seeing the older hotels inside the city.[12]

Contemporary Authorities

Rav Moshe Feinstein (*Teshuvot Igrot Moshe, Choshen Mishpat* 1:38) rules in accordance with the *Chatam Sofer* that one may not open a business if it will destroy someone else's livelihood. Rav Moshe rules that a loss of livelihood is not defined by a loss of one's home or his ability to put food on the table. Instead, he claims, taking away one's ability to afford as much as the average person in his socioeconomic class constitutes destroying his livelihood.[13] It should be noted that the case addressed by Rav Moshe also included other reasons to prohibit the new competition.[14]

Rav Ezra Basri (*Teshuvot Sha'arei Ezra* 2:131) does not quote the *Aviasaf*, although he does rule in accordance with the opinion of the Rashba (quoted above) that one may not lure away the original proprietor's regular customers.[15] Rav Basri permits selling *chametz* before *Pesach*[16] in a neighborhood where another rabbi has already been selling *chametz*, but he prohibits publicizing or advertising the rival business, so as not to take away regular customers from the first rabbi. Rav Basri adds that if any community establishes an official policy in these matters, the policy is halachically binding. For example, if the local Religious Affairs Councils in Israel were to appoint specific rabbis to sell *chametz*, this designation would preclude all other rabbis from running a competing sale.

Some authorities are even more lenient about competition. The *Beit Efraim* (C.M. 26) rules against the *Aviasaf*'s view, and the Tel Aviv Beit Din (*Piskei Din Rabbaniyim* 4:9-32) also leans this way. Rav Yosef Adler reports that Rav Yosef Dov Soloveitchik adopted a similar approach when an established kosher pizza store sought to block another pizza store from opening in the same area (Bergen County, New Jersey). The local rabbis (Rav Adler and Rav Macy Gordon) consulted with Rav Soloveitchik, who ruled in favor of the new entrepreneurs. The Rav insisted that in America there are no restrictions on competition, although he did not explain his reasoning.

There is also another possible reason to permit competition in America today. Murray Laulicht (a prominent Orthodox attorney) informed this author that almost all restrictions of economic activity violate civil antitrust statutes. This point may be significant, and the issue of whether *dina demalchuta dina* (the principle that the law of the land is halachically binding) applies in a given situation must be carefully examined.[17]

No clear consensus has emerged regarding rules for when to permit competition, so the ruling in each case depends upon the understanding of the particular *dayanim* involved.

Five Cases of Consensus

Although most issues of competition are subject to debate, there are at least five cases where nearly all authorities appear to agree.

I. Better Prices or Merchandise

The Rama (C.M. 156:7, based on the Ri Migash, quoted by the Tur, C.M. 156) rules that a new competitor may not be restricted if his prices or the quality of his merchandise are preferable for the Jewish consumers.[18] According to the *Aruch Hashulchan* (C.M. 156:11), this ruling also applies to a merchant who is selling different merchandise, even if his prices and quality are no better. However, the *Aruch Hashulchan* warns that the leniency toward a competitor with cheaper prices only applies if the competitor is not engaging in predatory pricing. If the old merchant was charging a high price, he explains, the new competitor may charge a more reasonable one. However, if the old merchant was charging a reasonable price, such that further lowering his price would prevent him from turning a profit, the new competitor may not open.

II. Necessary Monopolies

The *Chatam Sofer* (*Choshen Mishpat* 79) rules that communities should ensure that industries which require monopoly protection (i.e., protection from competition) receive it.[19] Rav Dr. Aaron Levine (*Free Enterprises and Jewish Law*, pp. 19-20) suggests that power companies and urban transportation are contemporary examples of enterprises that need monopoly protection in order to survive.[20] Some may argue that basic Jewish service providers in small Jewish communities similarly need monopoly protection to survive.[21]

III. Teaching Torah

The Gemara (*Bava Batra* 21b-22a) states that even Rav Huna permits unrestricted competition in the area of Torah education, since competition fosters improved Torah knowledge (*kin'at sofrim tarbeh chochmah*). This idea applies only to Torah study, but not to other religious services.[22] For example, Rav Ezra Basri (*Shaarei Ezra* 2:131) rules that the laws of *hasagat gevul* apply to the sale of *chametz* before *Pesach*, because *kinat sofrim tarbeh chochmah* only applies to teaching Torah per se. Even when competition is technically permissible between Torah scholars, Rav Basri (based on the *Chatam Sofer*'s conclusion) adds that rabbis must be extra strict about only competing fairly, to set a proper example for everyone else.

IV. Business Districts

Many contemporary authorities believe that a competing store occasionally enhances the business of the first storeowner. Under certain circumstances, the new store helps transform the area into a center for a certain type of businesses. Residents of Manhattan are familiar with garment districts, flower districts, furniture districts, and other similar commercial zones. Such areas attract large amounts of consumers, who spend more money than if they were patronizing a single store. Rav Moshe D. Tendler (in a lecture at Yeshiva University) and Rav Basri (personal communication) permit competition in such circumstances, as the original storeowners benefit from the newcomers.

V. Contemporary Neighborhoods

It should be noted that changing patterns in the geography of business impact halachic discussions of competition. Many businesses today do not cater exclusively to their local neighborhoods. For example, the

Tel Aviv Beit Din has written that competition between insurance agents should not be restricted according to the distinction between local residents and outsiders, as the insurance industry is not a neighborhood-based field (*Piskei Din Rabaniyim* 6:3). Following this reasoning, geographic location would not limit stores that conduct much of their business through the World Wide Web. Thus, each business must be individually evaluated, based on contemporary business conditions, to determine if the rules of *hasagat gevul* apply to it.

Conclusion

This area is particularly complex, as it depends on both many unresolved halachic disputes and changing business conditions. It is thus important to present all cases to *dayanim* who are Torah scholars and who understand the intricacies of business (see *Aruch Hashulchan*, C.M. 15:6). It should not surprise people to find that different *batei din* rule differently in these matters, considering the many unresolved disputes involved.

© 2000, Rabbi Howard Jachter

Footnotes

* This article is excerpted from the book *Gray Matter: Discourses in Contemporary Halachah*, by Rabbi Chaim Jachter with Ezra Frazer, and is reprinted with permission from the author .

1. For a discussion of how this term attained its modern usage, see Rav Simcha Krauss's essay in *The Journal of Halacha and Contemporary Society* (29:5-29).

2. See *Encyclopedia Talmudit* (1:62) for more details on this issue.

3. See Rashi, s.v. *Shani Dagim*, and *Nimukei Yosef, Bava Batra* 11a in pages of Rif s.v. *Bar Mevo'ah*; see *Teshuvot Chatam Sofer, Choshen Mishpat* 79, for a summary of alternative explanations of this passage.

4. An Israeli rabbinical court ruled that a "neighborhood" is the contemporary halachic equivalent of a Talmudic *mavuy* (*Piskei Din Rabbaniyim* 6:3).

5. *Yachid verabim Halachah kerabim*; see *Mo'eid Katan* 20a and *Tosafot* s.v. *Kol*.

6. *Halachah kevatrai*; see *Encyclopedia Talmudit* 9:341-345. In this case, Rav Huna the son of Rav Yehoshua lived later.

7. These Rishonim include the Rif (*Bava Batra* 11a in pages of Rif), *Tosafot* (*Bava Batra* 21b s.v. *Peshita*), the Rambam (*Hilchot Shecheinim* 6:8), and the Rosh (*Bava Batra* 2:12).

8. See Rif and *Nimukei Yosef* s.v. *Lo Chayat, Bava Batra* 11a in pages of Rif; Rosh, *Bava Batra* 2:12; and *Tur, Choshen Mishpat* 156.

9. The *Rishonim* also debate precisely what constitutes the necessary type of tax for this purpose. See the commentary attributed to Rabbeinu Gershom (*Bava Batra* 21b s.v. *Bar Mata*), *Hag'hot Ashri* (*Bava Batra* 2:12), *Bach* (C.M. 156 s.v. *Umah Shekatav Im*), *Beit Yosef* (C.M. 156 s.v *Hacheilek Hasheini*), and *Biur Hagra* (C.M. 156:23).

10. For purposes of clarity, we will refer to opinions that permit competition as lenient and ones that limit it as strict or stringent. Obviously, from the point of view of the original proprietor, the more "lenient" opinions cause greater hardship, while the more "stringent" ones benefit him.

11. Of course, the *Chatam Sofer* himself sharply attacks this claim and tries to prove that King David's eleven principles are all technically binding, just as the 613 *mitzvot*, which they symbolize, are all obligatory.

12. The *Pitchei Teshuvah* cites many authorities on each side of the debate regarding limiting competition.

13. The *Chatam Sofer* himself distinguishes between weakening someone's business ("*chulshat chiyuteih*") and totally ruining it ("*pisuk chiyuteih*"), and he only prohibits the latter. *Pisuk chiyuteih* could have been interpreted as driving the person into poverty, but Rav Moshe adduces a proof from the laws of *ribbit* (the prohibition to charge interest) that it should be understood more broadly.

14. The new competitors in this case were providing the same service as the incumbent, but they were not doing it for personal profit. Rav Moshe felt that their lack of interest in making money from the service made it less legitimate for them to ruin someone else's opportunity to earn a livelihood. They could not claim, "You do work on your home turf, and [so too] I do work on my home turf," because they did not need the work for their livelihood in the same way that their competitor did.

15. It should be noted that Rav Basri is a Sephardic authority, which might explain why he bases his ruling on the Rashba, a Sephardic *Rishon*, rather than the various Ashkenazic *Rishonim* and *Acharonim* quoted earlier in our chapter.

16. It is common for people to give some money to the rabbi who sells their *chametz* to a non-Jew.

17. This issue might hinge on the dispute between the *Rama* (C.M. 73:14) and the *Shach* (73:39). See Professor Steven Resnicoff's extensive review of the debate among halachic authorities as to whether Halachah should assimilate secular bankruptcy laws (*The Journal of Halacha and Contemporary Society* 24:5-54). Also see the fascinating debate between Rav Shlomo Dichovsky and Rav Avraham Sherman (*Techumin* (18:18-40 and 19:205-220) as to whether Halachah should assimilate secular equitable distribution laws.

18. In the Rama's responsum (10) prohibiting a second edition of the *Mishneh Torah*, the second edition was of worse quality than the first edition.

19. See *Teshuvot Igrot Moshe* (C.M. 2:39) regarding the negative effect of having rival organizations supervise *kashrut* in the same community. Rav Moshe instructs the local rabbinical council in Pittsburgh, Pennsylvania to maintain sole control of *kashrut* supervision.

20. At the time that this is being written, the issue of protecting a monopoly over power is being debated in parts of America, and protecting a monopoly over public transportation is a matter of great debate in Israel.

21. Ezra Frazer points out that such a situation may be analogous to a case addressed by the *Chatam Sofer* (C.M. 61). Two people were vying for the job of town butcher, one who had held the position for a long time and one who had substituted for this butcher and now wanted to be a butcher himself. The *Chatam Sofer* takes into consideration that the town was not capable of supporting two butchers as a reason to rule against the newer candidate. (In the end, he rules in favor of the newer candidate due to certain unique circumstances surrounding the specific people involved.)

22. See *Chatam Sofer, Choshen Mishpat* 19 and 79 s.v. *Mah*.

http://www.jlaw.com/Articles/hasagatgevul.html

Acknowledgments

The course before you is a revision of the course, *Talmudic Ethics,* which was first offered by the **Rohr Jewish Learning Institute** in Fall 2003. **Rabbi Moshe Miller** was the co-author of the original course, and Lessons 2 and 6 in particular bear the strong imprint of his work. The original *Talmudic Ethics* was the first course I authored for **JLI,** and **Rabbi Chaim Zalman Levy** provided considerable guidance in inducting me into the **JLI** writing culture.

We have been fortunate to have an outstanding editorial board guiding this revision. My thanks go to **Rabbi Levi Kaplan, Rabbi Yakov Latowicz, Rabbi Yosef Loschak,** and **Rabbi Peretz Shapiro**, for their incisive and thoughtful comments. Special thanks to **Rabbi Kaplan** as well for the proofing of the Hebrew texts and his review of the final document.

I gratefully acknowledge **Akiva Silberstein's** comments on Lessons 5 and 6.

Mrs. Ya'akovah Weber meticulously copyedited the document. Thanks to **Nachman Levine** for the beautiful design as well as many thoughtful corrections to the text, and to **Shimon Leib Jacobs** for the printing.

I am grateful to the staff at **JLI** Central for their assistance with the production of the book: **JLI's** director, **Rabbi Efraim Mintz,** whose vision and oversight are a constant source of inspiration; **Rabbi Mendel Sirota** and **Rabbi Mendel Bell** for technical support; **Mrs. Mindy Wallach** and **Mrs. Rivka Sternberg** for administrative assistance; and **Rabbi Yoni Katz** who has done much to aid our final production.

I am indebted to **jlaw.com** for the majority of the additional readings in the student textbooks.

Finally, my gratitude to our principal patron, **Rabbi Moshe Kotlarsky,** and to our primary benefactors, **George and Pamela Rohr.** Their enthusiastic support of the work of the **Rohr Jewish Learning Institute** has made possible its phenomenal growth.

Rabbi Eli Silberstein

Chof Hey Adar Bet, 5768

Ithaca, New York

The **Rohr Jewish Learning Institute**

An affiliate of
Merkos L'Inyonei Chinuch
The Educational Arm of
The Chabad Lubavitch Movement
822 Eastern Parkway, Brooklyn, NY 11213

Rohr **JLI** Affiliates

Share the **Rohr JLI** experience with friends and relatives worldwide

ALABAMA

BIRMINGHAM
Rabbi Yossi Friedman
205.970.0100

ARIZONA

CHANDLER
Rabbi Mendel Deitsch
480.855.4333

GLENDALE
Rabbi Sholom Lew
602.375.2422

PHOENIX
Rabbi Zalman Levertov
Rabbi Yossi Friedman
602.944.2753

SCOTTSDALE
Rabbi Yossi Levertov
Rabbi Yossi Bryski
480.998.1410

CALIFORNIA

AGOURA HILLS
Rabbi Moshe Bryski
Rabbi Yisroel Levin
Rabbi Shlomo Bistritzky
818.991.0991

BAKERSFIELD
Rabbi Shmuel Schlanger
661.835.8381

BEL AIR
Rabbi Chaim Mentz
310.475.5311

BRENTWOOD
Rabbi Boruch Hecht
Rabbi Mordechai Zaetz
310.826.4453

BURBANK
Rabbi Shmuly Kornfeld
818.954.0070

CARLSBAD
Rabbi Yeruchem Eilfort
Rabbi Michoel Shapiro
760.943.8891

CHATSWORTH
Rabbi Yossi Spritzer
818.718.0777

CUPERTINO
Rabbi Reuven Goldstein
408.725.0910

EL MAR
Rabbi Tzvi Hirsch Piekarski
755.1886

GLENDALE
Rabbi Simcha Backman
818.240.2750

HUNTINGTON BEACH
Rabbi Aron Berkowitz
714.846.2285

IRVINE
Rabbi Alter Tenenbaum
Rabbi Elly Andrusier
949.786.5000

LOS FELIZ
Rabbi Leibel Korf
323.660.5177

MARINA DEL REY
Rabbi Danny Yiftach
Rabbi Mendy Avtzon
310.859.0770

MILL VALLEY
Rabbi Hillel Scop
415.381.3794

MISSION VIEJO
Rabbi Zalman Aron Kantor
949.770.1270

MONTEREY
Rabbi Dovid Holtzberg
831.643.2770

MT. OLYMPUS
Rabbi Sholom Ber Rodal
323-650-1444

NEWHALL
Rabbi Elchonon Marosov
661.254.3434

NEWPORT BEACH
Rabbi Reuven Mintz
949.721.9800

NORTH HOLLYWOOD
Rabbi Nachman Abend
818.989.9539

NORTHRIDGE
Rabbi Eli Rivkin
818.368.3937

PACIFIC PALISADES
Rabbi Zushe Cunin
310.454.7783

PASADENA
Rabbi Chaim Hanoka
626.564.8820

RANCHO CUCAMONGA
Rabbi Sholom B. Harlig
909.949.4553

RANCHO PALOS VERDES
Rabbi Yitzchok Magalnic
310.544.5544

REDONDO BEACH
Rabbi Dovid Lisbon
310.214.4999

SACRAMENTO
Rabbi Mendy Cohen
916.455.1400

S. BARBARA
Rabbi Yosef Loschak
805.683.1544

S. CLEMENTE
Rabbi Menachem M. Slavin
949.489.0723

S. CRUZ
Rabbi Yochanan Friedman
831.454.0101

S. DIEGO
Rabbi Motte Fradkin
858.547.0076

S. FRANCISCO
Rabbi Peretz Mochkin
415.571.8770

S. JOSE
Rabbi Aaron Cunin
408.358.5530

S. MONICA
Rabbi Boruch Rabinowitz
310.394.5699

S. RAFAEL
Rabbi Yisrael Rice
415.492.1666

S. ROSA
Rabbi Mendel Wolvovsky
707.577.0277

SIMI VALLEY
Rabbi Nosson Gurary
805.577.0573

STOCKTON
Rabbi Avremel Brod
209.952.2081

STUDIO CITY
Rabbi Yossi Baitelman
818.508.6633

TEMECULA
Rabbi Yitzchok Hurwitz
951.303.9576

THOUSAND OAKS
Rabbi Chaim Bryski
805.493.7776

TUSTIN
Rabbi Yehoshua Eliezrie
714.508.2150

VENTURA
Rabbi Yakov Latowicz
Mrs. Sarah Latowicz
805.658.7441

WEST HILLS
Rabbi Avrahom Yitzchak Rabin
818.337.4544

YORBA LINDA
Rabbi Dovid Eliezrie
714.693.0770

COLORADO
ASPEN
Rabbi Mendel Mintz
970.544.3770

BOULDER
Rabbi Pesach Scheiner
303.494.1638

COLORADO SPRINGS
Rabbi Moshe Liberow
719.634.2345

DENVER
Rabbi Yossi Serebryanski
303.744.9699

HIGHLANDS RANCH
Rabbi Avraham Mintz
303.694.9119

CONNECTICUT
BRANFORD
Rabbi Yossi Yaffe
203.488.2263

GLASTONBURY
Rabbi Yosef Wolvovsky
860.659.2422

GREENWICH
Rabbi Yossi Deren
Rabbi Menachem Feldman
203.629.9059

LITCHFIELD
Rabbi Yoseph Eisenbach
860.567.3609

NEW LONDON
Rabbi Avrohom Sternberg
860.437.8000

STAMFORD
Rabbi Yisrael Deren
Rabbi Levi Mendelow
203.3.CHABAD

WESTPORT
Rabbi Yehuda L. Kantor
Mrs. Dina Kantor
203.226.8584

WEST HARTFORD
Rabbi Yosef Gopin
Rabbi Shaya Gopin
860.659.2422

DELAWARE
WILMINGTON
Rabbi Chuni Vogel
302.529.9900

FLORIDA
AVENTURA
Rabbi Laivi Forta
Rabbi Chaim I. Drizin
305.933.0770

BAL HARBOUR
Rabbi Mendy Levy
305.868.1411

BOCA RATON
Rabbi Moishe Denberg
Rabbi Zalman Bukiet
561.417.7797

EAST BOCA RATON
Rabbi Ruvi New
561.417.7797

BOYNTON BEACH
Rabbi Yosef Yitzchok Raichik
561.732.4633

BRADENTON
Rabbi Menachem Bukiet
941.388.9656

BRANDON
Rabbi Mendel Rubashkin
813.657.9393

COCONUT CREEK
Rabbi Yossi Gansburg
954.422.1987

FORT LAUDERDALE
Rabbi Yitzchok Naparstek
954.568.1190

FORT MYERS
Rabbi Yitzchok Minkowicz
Mrs. Nechama Minkowicz
239.433.7708

HOLLYWOOD
Rabbi Leizer Barash
954.965.9933

Rabbi Yossi Korf
Rabbi Yakov Garfinkel
954.967.8341

KENDALL
Rabbi Yossi Harlig
305.234.5654

KEY BISCAYNE
Rabbi Yoel Caroline
305.365.6744

KEY WEST
Rabbi Yaakov Zucker
305.295.0013

MIAMI DOWNTOWN
Rabbi Chaim Lipskar
786.368.9040

NAPLES
Rabbi Fishel Zaklos
239.262.4474

NORTH MIAMI BEACH
Rabbi Moishe Kievman
305.770.1919

PALM HARBOR
Rabbi Shalom Adler
727.789.0408

PARKLAND
Rabbi Mendy Gutnik
954.796.7330

S. PETERSBURG
Rabbi Alter Korf
727.344.4900

SARASOTA
Rabbi Chaim Shaul Steinmetz
941.925.0770
SUNNY ISLES BEACH
Rabbi Yisrael Baron
CLASSES IN ENGLISH
305.792.4770

SUNNY ISLES BEACH
Rabbi Alexander Kaller
CLASSES IN RUSSIAN
305.803.5315

TALLAHASSEE
Rabbi Schneur Zalmen Oirechman
850.523.9294

VENICE
Rabbi Sholom Ber Schmerling
941.493.2770

WELLINGTON
Rabbi Menachem Mendel Muskal
561.753.2220

WESTON
Rabbi Yisroel Spalter
Rabbi Yechezkel Unsdorfer
954.349.6565

WEST PALM BEACH
Rabbi Yoel Gancz
561.659.7770

GEORGIA
ALPHARETTA
Rabbi Hirshy Minkowicz
770.410.9000

ATLANTA
Rabbi Yossi New
Rabbi Isser New
404.843.2464

ATLANTA: INTOWN
Rabbi Eliyahu Schusterman
Rabbi Ari Sollish
404.898.0434

GWINNETT
Rabbi Yossi Lerman
678.595.0196

MARIETTA
Rabbi Ephraim Silverman
770.565.4412

IDAHO
BOISE
Rabbi Mendel Lifshitz
208.853.9200

ILLINOIS
CHICAGO
Rabbi Boruch Hertz
773.743.5434

Rabbi Meir Hecht
312.714.4655

GLENVIEW
Rabbi Yishaya Benjaminson
847.998.9896

HIGHLAND PARK
Mrs. Michla Schanowitz
847.266.0770

NORTHBROOK
Rabbi Meir Moscowitz
847.564.8770

PEORIA
Rabbi Eli Langsam
309.692.2250

SKOKIE
Rabbi Yochanan Posner
847.677.1770

WILMETTE
Rabbi Dovid Flinkenstein
847.251.7707

INDIANA
INDIANAPOLIS
Rabbi Mendel Schusterman
317.251.5573

KANSAS
OVERLAND PARK
Rabbi Mendy Wineberg
913.649.4852

LOUISIANA
METAIRIE
Rabbi Yossi Nemes
504.454.2910

MARYLAND
ANNAPOLIS
Rabbi Nochum Light
443.321.4628

BALTIMORE
Rabbi Elchonon Lisbon
410.358.4787

COLUMBIA
Rabbi Hillel Baron
410.740.2424

GAITHERSBURG
Rabbi Sholom Raichik
1.926.3632

POTOMAC
Rabbi Mendel Bluming
301.983.4200

Silver Spring
Rabbi Berel Wolvovsky
301.593.1117

MASSACHUSETTS
ANDOVER
Rabbi Asher Bronstein
978.470.2288

THE BERKSHIRES
Rabbi Levi Volovik
413.499.9899

CHESTNUT HILL
Rabbi Mendy Uminer
617.738.9770

HYANNIS
Rabbi Yekusiel Alperowitz
508.775.2324

LONGMEADOW
Rabbi Yakov Wolff
413.567.8665

NATICK
Rabbi Levi Fogelman
508.650.1499

SHARON
Rabbi Chaim Wolosow
Rabbi Ilan Meyers
781.784.4269

SUDBURY
Rabbi Yisroel Freeman
978.443.3691

SWAMPSCOTT
Mrs. Layah Lipsker
781.581.3833

MICHIGAN
ANN ARBOR
Rabbi Aharon Goldstein
734.995.3276

WEST BLOOMFIELD
Rabbi Kasriel Shemtov
248.788.4000
Rabbi Elimelech Silberberg
Rabbi Avrohom Wineberg
248.855 .6170

MINNESOTA
MINNETONKA
Rabbi Mordechai Grossbaum
952.929.9922

MISSOURI
ST. LOUIS
Rabbi Yosef Landa
314.725.0400

NEVADA
LAS VEGAS
Rabbi Shea Harlig
Rabbi Tzvi Bronstein
702.259.0770

SUMMERLIN
Rabbi Yisroel Schanowitz
Rabbi Tzvi Bronstein
702.855.0770

NEW JERSEY
BASKING RIDGE
Rabbi Mendy Herson
908.604.8844

CHERRY HILL
Rabbi Mendy Mangel
856.874.1500

CLINTON
Rabbi Eli Kornfeld
908.623.7000

FORT LEE
Rabbi Meir Konikov
201.886.1238

FRANKLIN LAKES
Rabbi Chanoch Kaplan
201.848.0449

HILLSBOROUGH
Rabbi Shmaya Krinsky
908.874.0444

HOBOKEN
Rabbi Moshe Shapiro
201.386.5222

MANALAPAN
Rabbi Boruch Chazanow
732.972.3687

MARGATE
Rabbi Avrohom Rapoport
609.822.8500

MEDFORD
Rabbi Yitzchok Kahan
609.953.3150

NORTH BRUNSWICK
Rabbi Levi Azimov
732.398.9492

RANDOLPH
Rabbi Avraham Bechor
973.895.3070

ROCKAWAY
Rabbi Asher Herson
Rabbi Mordechai Baumgarten
973.625.1525

SCOTCH PLAINS
Rabbi Avrohom Blesofsky
908.790.0008

TEANECK
Rabbi Ephraim Simon
201.907.0686

TENAFLY
Rabbi Mordechai Shain
Rabbi Chaim Boyarsky
201.871.1152

TOMS RIVER
Rabbi Moshe Gourarie
732.349.4199

WAYNE
Rabbi Michel Gurkov
973.694.6274

WEST ORANGE
Rabbi Efraim Mintz
Rabbi Mendy Kasowitz
973.731.0770

WOODCLIFF LAKE
Rabbi Dov Drizin
201.476.0157

NEW MEXICO
SANTA FE
Rabbi Berel Levertov
505.983.2000

NEW YORK
ALBANY
Rabbi Yossi Rubin
518.482.5781

BEDFORD
Rabbi Arik Wolf
914.666.6065

BINGHAMTON
Mrs. Rivkah Slonim
607.797.0015

BRIGHTON BEACH
Rabbi Zushe Winner
Rabbi Avrohom Winner
718.946.9833

BROOKLYN HEIGHTS
Rabbi Aaron Raskin
718.596.4840 X11

BUFFALO
Rabbi Moshe Gurary
716.578.1136

CEDARHURST
Rabbi Shneur Zalman Wolowik
516.295.2478

CROWN HEIGHTS
Rabbi Levi Kaplan
Mrs. Shimona Tzukernik
718.221.6900

DIX HILLS
Rabbi Yackov Saacks
631.351.8672

DOBBS FERRY
Rabbi Benjy Silverman
914.693.6100

GLEN HEAD
Rabbi Mendy Heber
516.671.6620

ITHACA
Rabbi Eli Silberstein
607.257.7379

KINGSTON
Rabbi Yitzchok Hecht
845.334.9044

NYC GRAMERCY PARK
Rabbi Naftali Rotenstreich
212.924.3200

NYC KEHILATH JESHURUN
Rabbi Elie Weinstock
212.774.5636

NYC WASHINGTON SQUARE
Rabbi Yaakov Bankhalter
Rabbi Shmuel Kravitsky
212.627.3270

OSSINING
Rabbi Dovid Labkowski
914.923.2522

PARK SLOPE
Rabbi Levi Kaplan
718.832.1266

RIVERDALE
Rabbi Levi Shemtov
718.549.1100

ROCHESTER
Rabbi Nechemia Vogel
585.271.0330

ROSLYN
Rabbi Yaakov Reiter
516.484.8185

SCARSDALE
Rabbi Velvl Butman
914.723.2422

SEA GATE
Rabbi Chaim Brikman
Mrs. Rivka Brikman
718.266.1736

STONY BROOK
Rabbi Shalom Ber Cohen
631.585.0521

WOODBURY
Rabbi Shmuel Lipszyc
516.682.0404

NORTH CAROLINA
ASHEVILLE
Rabbi Shaya Susskind
828.505.0746

CHARLOTTE
Rabbi Yossi Groner
Rabbi Shlomo Cohen
704.366.3984

RALEIGH
Rabbi Aaron Herman
919.637.6950

OHIO
BEACHWOOD
Rabbi Yossi Marosov
216.381.4736

BLUE ASH
Rabbi Yisroel Mangel
513.793.5200

COLUMBUS
Rabbi Areyah Kaltmann
Rabbi Levi Andrusier
614.294.3296

DAYTON
Rabbi Nochum Mangel
Rabbi Dr. Shmuel Klatzkin
937.643.0770

TOLEDO
Rabbi Yossi Shemtov
419.843.9393

OKLAHOMA
OKLAHOMA CITY
Rabbi Ovadia Goldman
405.524.4800

TULSA
Rabbi Yehuda Weg
918.492.4499

OREGON
PORTLAND
Rabbi Moshe Wilhelm
Rabbi Mordechai Wilhelm
503.977.9947

PENNSYLVANIA
AMBLER
Rabbi Shaya Deitsch
215.591.9310

BALA CYNWYD
Rabbi Shraga Sherman
610.660.9192

CLARKS SUMMIT
Rabbi Benny Rapoport
570.587.3300

DEVON
Rabbi Yossi Kaplan
610.971.9977

FOX CHAPEL
Rabbi Ely Rosenfeld
412.781.1800

LANCASTER
Rabbi Elazar Green
717.368.6565

NEWTOWN
Rabbi Aryeh Weinstein
215.497.9925

PHILADELPHIA: CENTER CITY
Rabbi Yochonon Goldman
215.238.2100

PITTSBURGH
Rabbi Yisroel Altein
412.422.7300 ext. 269

PITTSBURGH: SOUTH HILLS
Rabbi Mendy Rosenblum
412.278.3693

SHADYSIDE
Rabbi Mordy Rudolph
412.363.2422

STROUDSBURG
Rabbi Mendel Bendet
570.420.8655

RHODE ISLAND
BARRINGTON
Rabbi Moshe Laufer
401.273.7238

SOUTH CAROLINA
COLUMBIA
Rabbi Hesh Epstein
803.782.1831

TENNESSEE
BELLEVUE
Rabbi Yitzchok Tiechtel
615.646.5750

KNOXVILLE
Rabbi Yossi Wilhelm
865.588.8584

MEMPHIS
Rabbi Levi Klein
901.766.1800

TEXAS
DALLAS
Rabbi Mendel Dubrawsky
Rabbi Zvi Drizin
Rabbi Peretz Shapiro
972.818.0770

FORT WORTH
Rabbi Dov Mandel
817.361.7704

HOUSTON
Rabbi Moishe Traxler
Rabbi Dovid Goldstein
713.774.0300

HOUSTON: RICE UNIVERSITY AREA
Rabbi Eliezer Lazaroff
Rabbi Yitzchok Schmukler
713.522.2004

PLANO
Rabbi Mendel Block
Rabbi Yehudah Horowitz
972.596.8270

S. ANTONIO
Rabbi Chaim Block
Rabbi Yossi Marrus
10.492.1085

VIRGINA
ALEXANDRIA/ARLINGTON
Rabbi Mordechai Newman
703.370.2774

FAIRFAX
Rabbi Leibel Fajnland
703.426.1980

NORFOLK
Rabbi Aaron Margolin
Rabbi Levi Brashevitzky
757.616.0770

RICHMOND
Rabbi Dr. Shlomo Pereira
804.740.2000

TYSONS CORNER
Rabbi Levi Deitsch
703.356.3451

WASHINGTON
SEATTLE
Rabbi Elazar Bogomilsky
206.527.1411

WISCONSIN
MEQUON
Rabbi Menachem Rapoport
262.242.2235

MILWAUKEE
Rabbi Mendel Shmotkin
Rabbi Shais Taub
414.961.6100

AUSTRALIA
BRISBANE
Rabbi Chanoch Sufrin
617.3843.6770

MELBOURNE
Rabbi Shimshon Yurkowicz
613.9822.3600

PERTH
Rabbi Shalom White
618.9275.2106

SYDNEY
BONDI
Rabbi Pinchas Feldman
612.9387.3822

DOUBLE BAY
Rabbi Yanky Berger
612.9327.1644

DOVER HEIGHTS
Rabbi Benzion Milecki
612.9337.6775

NORTH SHORE
Rabbi Nochum Schapiro
Mrs. Fruma Schapiro
Rabbi Shmuly Kopel
612.9488.9548

AUSTRIA
VIENNA
Rabbi Shaya Boas
431.369.1818 ext. 123

BELGIUM
ANTWERP
Rabbi Mendy Gurary
32.3.239.6212

BRAZIL
S. PAULO
Rabbi Avraham Steinmetz
55.11.3081.3081

CANADA
ALBERTA
CALGARY
Rabbi Mordechai Groner
403.238.4880

BRITISH COLUMBIA
RICHMOND
Rabbi Yechiel Baitelman
604.277.6427

VICTORIA
Rabbi Meir Kaplan
250.595.7656

ONTARIO
LONDON
Rabbi Eliezer Gurkow
519.434.3962

OTTAWA
Rabbi Menachem M. Blum
613.823.0866

GREATER TORONTO
REGIONAL OFFICE & THORNHILL
Rabbi Yossi Gansburg
905.731.7000

LAWRENCE/EGLINTON
Rabbi Menachem Gansburg
416.546.8770

MARKHAM
Rabbi Avraham E. Plotkin
905.886.0420

MIDTOWN
Rabbi Shlomo Wolvovsky
416.516.2005

MISSISSAUGA
Rabbi Yitzchok Slavin
905.820.4432

UPTOWN
Rabbi Moshe Steiner
647.267.8533

QUEBEC
HAMPSTEAD
Rabbi Moishe New
Rabbi Zalman Kaplan
514.342.1770

Montreal
Rabbi Berel Bell
Rabbi Ronnie Fine
Rabbi Leibel Fine
514.342.3.JLI

Town of Mount Royal
Rabbi Moshe Krasnanski
514.739.0770

COLOMBIA
Bogota
Rabbi Yehoshua B. Rosenfeld
Rabbi Chanoch Piekarski
571.635.8251

DENMARK
Copenhagen
Rabbi Yitzchok Lowenthal
45.3316.1850

GUATEMALA
Guatemala City
Rabbi Shalom Pelman
502.2485.0770

FINLAND
Helsinki
Rabbi Benyamin Wolff
358.9.278.1770

NETHERLANDS
Den Haag
Rabbi Shmuel Katzman
31.70.347.0222

Rotterdam
Rabbi Yehuda Vorst
31.10.466.9481

PANAMA
Panama
Rabbi Gabriel Benayon
507.223.3383

PUERTO RICO
Carolina
Rabbi Mendel Zarchi
787.253.0894

RUSSIA
Moscow
Rabbi Shneor Leider
Rabbi Yanky Klein
749.5783.8479

SOUTH AFRICA
Cape Town
Rabbi Mendel Popack
Rabbi Pinchas Hecht
27.21.434.3740

Johannesburg
Rabbi Dovid Masinter
Rabbi Yossi Hecht
Rabbi Daniel Rabin
27.11.440.6600

SWEDEN
Stockholm
Rabbi Chaim Greisman
468.679.7067

UNITED KINGDOM
Cheadle
Rabbi Peretz Chein
44.161.428.1818

London
Rabbi Gershon Overlander
Rabbi Dovid Katz
502.2485.0770

Manchester
Rabbi Chaim Farro
44.161.795.4000

Leeds
Rabbi Eli Pink
44.113.266.3311

URUGUAY
Montevideo
Rabbi Eliezer Shemtov
5982.709.3444 ext. 109/110

VENEZUELA
Caracas
Rabbi Yehoshua Rosenblum
58.212.264.7011

Notes

Notes

Marketing Committee
Rabbi Chaim Block
Chairman
San Antonio, TX

Rabbi Mendy Halberstam
Coordinator
Miami, FL

Rabbi Yehuda Shemtov
Yardley, PA

Rabbi Simcha Backman
Glendale, CA

Rabbi Ronnie Fine
Montreal, QC

Rabbi Ovadiah Goldman
Oklahoma City, OK

Marketing Consultants
Gary Wexler
Passion Marketing
Los Angeles, CA

Tzvi Freeman
Toronto, ON

JJ Gross
Blowdart Advertising & Marketing
New York, NY

Alan Rosenspan
Newton, MA

Online Division
Rabbi Mendel Bell
Rabbi Mendel Sirota

Administration
Rabbi Yoni Katz
Rabbi Mendel Sirota
Rabbi Mendy Weg

Affiliate Support
Rabbi Levi Brod
Rabbi Mendel Sirota

Affiliate Liaisons
Rivka Sternberg
Nechama Shmotkin
Mindy Wallach

Publication Design
Nachman Levine
Detroit, MI

Research Editor
Nachman Levine

Copy Editors
Ya'akova Weber
Brooklyn, NY

Al Miller
Manalapan, NJ

Graphic Design
Gershon Eichorn
Zalman Stock
Yitzchok Goldberg
Spotlight Design, NY

Accounting
Nechama Shmotkin
Shaina B. Mintz

Printing
Lorne Jacobs
Point One Communications
Montreal, QC

Multimedia Development
Rabbi Benny Rapoport
Rabbi Chesky Edelman
Rabbi Mendel Rivkin
Rabbi Levi Teldon
Dr. Chana Silberstein

JLI Departments

Torah Studies
Rabbi Yossi Gansburg
Chairman
Toronto, ON

Rabbi Meir Hecht
Director

Rabbi Yechezkel Deitsch
Administrator

Sinai Scholars Society
Rabbi Menachem Schmidt
Chairman
Philadelphia, PA

Rabbi Moshe Chaim Dubrowski
Chabad on Campus

Rabbi Yitzchok Dubov
Director

Rabbi Lev Cotlar
Affiliate Liasion

myShiur:
Advanced Learning Initiative
Rabbi Shmuel Kaplan
Chairman
Baltimore, MD

Rabbi Levi Kaplan
Director

National Jewish Retreat
Rabbi Heshy Epstein
Chairman
Columbia, SC

Rabbi Mendy Weg
Coordinator

JLI Teacher Training and e-Learning
Rabbi Berel Bell
Director

Rabbi Shaya Smetana
Coordinator

JLI For Teens
Rabbi Benny Rapoport
Director

JLI International Desk
Rabbi Moshe Heber
Coordinator

Notes

Notes

Notes